How to Thrive in RETROGRADE

Pavilion
An imprint of HarperCollins*Publishers* Ltd
1 London Bridge Street
London SE1 9GF

www.harpercollins.co.uk

HarperCollins*Publishers*
Macken House
39/40 Mayor Street Upper,
Dublin 1
D01 C9W8
Ireland

10 9 8 7 6 5 4 3 2 1

First published in Great Britain by Pavilion
An imprint of HarperCollins*Publishers* 2025

Copyright © Pavilion 2025
Written by Alison Davies

The author asserts the moral right to be identified as the author of this work.
A catalogue record of this book is available from the British Library.

ISBN 978-0-00-875272-9

Publishing Director: Laura Russell
Commissioning Editor: Caitlin Doyle
Editor: Shamar Gunning
Cover and interior designer: maru studio G.K.
Illustrations © shutterstock.com
Production Controller: Grace O'Byrne
Copyeditor: Helena Caldon
Proofreader: Rachel Malig
Indexer: Vanessa Bird
Production: Grace O'Byrne

Printed and bound by PNB Print in Latvia

All rights reserved. No part of this publication may be reproduced, stored in a retrieval system, or transmitted, in any form or by any means, electronic, mechanical, photocopying, recording or otherwise, without the prior written permission of the publishers.

Without limiting the author's and publisher's exclusive rights, any unauthorized use of this publication to train generative artificial intelligence (AI) technologies is expressly prohibited. HarperCollins also exercise their rights under Article 4(3) of the Digital Single Market Directive 2019/790 and expressly reserve this publication from the text and data mining exception.

This book contains FSC™ certified paper and other controlled sources to ensure responsible forest management.

For more information visit: www.harpercollins.co.uk/green

ALISON DAVIES

How to Thrive in RETROGRADE

Navigate the chaos and
live in cosmic harmony

PAVILION

I would like to dedicate this book to Dorothy Holland, who always had a fascination with the stars and the corresponding zodiac signs.

CONTENTS

Introduction — 6

RETROGRADE: WHAT IT IS AND
WHAT IT MEANS FOR YOU — 10

PLANET PROFILES — 46

RETROGRADE PLANETS AND
YOUR STAR SIGN — 104

THE RETROGRADES AND HOW
TO WORK WITH THEM — 152

PLANETS IN RETROGRADE DIARY — 201

Further Reading and Resources — 208
Glossary — 212
Index — 216
Acknowledgements — 221
Author Bio — 222

INTRODUCTION

Since the dawn of time, humans have been fascinated with the night sky. We have looked to the stars for heavenly inspiration, gasping in awe at their beauty. We have pondered this celestial backdrop and the secrets it holds, imagining new worlds and vistas of potential in the scene that sweeps overhead. We have made up stories to explain the planets and their movements, given them names and attributes that fit with mythological narratives and the way they appear. After all, it is human nature to make sense of the world around us, to put labels on things and try to create a sense of order out of chaos.

The planets in our galaxy first came to the attention of ancient civilizations thousands of years ago, but those early efforts were based purely on what the naked eye could see from Earth. Even so, the skies were studied in depth and charted by the Assyro-Babylonians around 1000 BCE. They researched the stars and charted their movements, building up a body of knowledge that formed the basis of modern astronomy. It was around the 3rd century BCE that the Greeks intervened, using astrometry to estimate cosmic scales and get a better understanding of how far away the planets were. The Romans were quick to get on board, naming each planet after one of their gods, based on qualities such as how big it was (Jupiter) or how brightly it shone in the night sky (Venus), and because Latin was the language of most of those early astronomers, it made sense that the names were Roman rather than Greek.

The order of movement of the cosmos was a subject that mystified many of those early scholars. Famous Greek philosophers Plato and Aristotle claimed the cosmos moved in perfect circles, but this theory didn't explain the supposed 'backward' movement of retrograde motion, a phenomenon that must have astounded the Ancients.

It was the astronomer Ptolemy who first introduced the concept of retrograde and prograde movement in around 150 CE. Believing that the Earth was the centre of the Solar System, he used a series of offset circles to explain the forward and backward motion of the planets, and while this remained the prominent view until the Renaissance, there were many who picked holes in his hypothesis.

Luckily, the introduction of the telescope put everything into perspective, so now we know so much more about what goes on above our heads. Thousands of years of research have given us a detailed insight into the movement of the stars, planets, and moons that make up the Solar System and how they influence our daily life. We can appreciate those early narratives and understand how the planets might affect us by looking in detail at our birth charts. But while we are all born under a specific sign of the zodiac, there is still more to learn when it comes to the power of the planets and how they figure in our fate.

This book takes you on a journey through the starry skies, introducing the main inner and outer planets that those early astronomers established as part of the Solar System. You will discover each one's attributes, the mystical gifts and associations that are linked to the planet, and its specific themes. You will learn how to connect with the planet's energy and work with it during retrograde motion – a particularly powerful time that can be harnessed with life-changing results! Tips and rituals are provided to help you prepare for any type of retrograde, along with more in-depth rituals and self-care activities that you can carry out during each planet's backspin. You will learn how to go with the ebb and flow of the cosmos, which in turn will help you connect with the Universe at a much deeper level.

Peppered with fascinating facts about the way the Solar System works, this book will help you understand the movements of the stars, and how their orbit can bring profound gains to your life. The retrograde diary provides an overview of the planets' movements over the next five years, allowing you to prepare for each specific energy phase. Arranged in easy-to-read chapters that can be digested in order or dipped into for advice depending on the starscape at the time, *The Power of Retrograde* is your go-to guide for tapping into planet power!

CHAPTER ONE

RETROGRADE: WHAT IT IS & WHAT IT MEANS FOR YOU

Ancient astronomers believed that when each planet went into retrograde it was retreating to the mythical Underworld, where, immersed in darkness, it would face a range of challenges and tests to overcome the force of evil. When it returned full cycle and began moving forwards, its energy was renewed – invigorated by time spent in the shadow realm. While we now understand that retrograde is an astrological illusion and the planets don't actually go anywhere, the concept of going within the bosom of the Earth is one that has stuck.

Retrogrades can set us back; indeed, they encourage us to reflect upon the past and face issues that we have swept aside by putting us in a state of flux, but this is the source of their gift. When everything appears to be moving forwards in a steady flow, it's easy to pretend, to bury concerns and fears without fully addressing them. Retrogrades are an opportunity to stop what we're doing and tie up loose ends, by facing them head on. While these retrogrades can cause chaos, it is within this unpredictable landscape that we learn and grow, so while we don't actually descend into the Underworld, we do have a regression of sorts and a journey to take.

This chapter puts the focus on retrograde energy, what it is, and how we can work with it, by examining what it means when a planet appears to spin backwards, and how we can prepare for the resulting challenges ahead. Suggestions and practical tips are outlined to help you harness retrograde energy and avoid the common pitfalls. Whatever your star sign and whichever planet is in retrograde, you will benefit from a little time out and some simple planning.

WHAT A PLANET IN RETROGRADE MEANS

When a planet is in retrograde it appears to be moving backwards in the sky, but this is an optical illusion. Planets always revolve around the Sun in the same direction, going west to east in a movement called prograde. In reality, retrograde motion happens when the planet is in close proximity to the Earth, making it look like it's going backwards instead of forwards. Each planet orbits the Sun at a different speed, and when a faster-moving planet passes a slower one, from our perspective on Earth the slower planet 'appears' to be reversing.

And this is all about the point of perspective and your location at the time of stargazing. Every planet has the potential to go into retrograde when viewed from another, so while the Earth maintains a prograde rotation and orbit of the Sun, it could potentially appear in retrograde when looked at from another planet.

Like any backward motion, this has an effect on the way we view things, causing us to look inwards and reflect upon different areas of our life. It's an opportunity to backtrack, and like the planet, go within ourselves and seek clarification and peace. Although retrograde planets have a reputation for being disruptive for us here on Earth, this disruption provides stargazers with a positive opportunity for growth and transformation, depending on the planet and where it sits in your astrological sign.

Most of the time planets move forwards, which means that when a planet is in retrograde, it's going off the beaten track and doing something unusual. It's no surprise, then, that this affects the way you think and feel. Some planets, like Mercury, Venus, and Mars, move closer to the Earth when they're in retrograde, making their presence even more powerful, which means you experience the effects at a very personal level. While this might bring challenges, it also provides some major opportunities for change and rejuvenation. To make the most of these, you need to be aware of what each retrograde means and the influence this has on your sign. You can then embrace the energy and use it to manifest positive change.

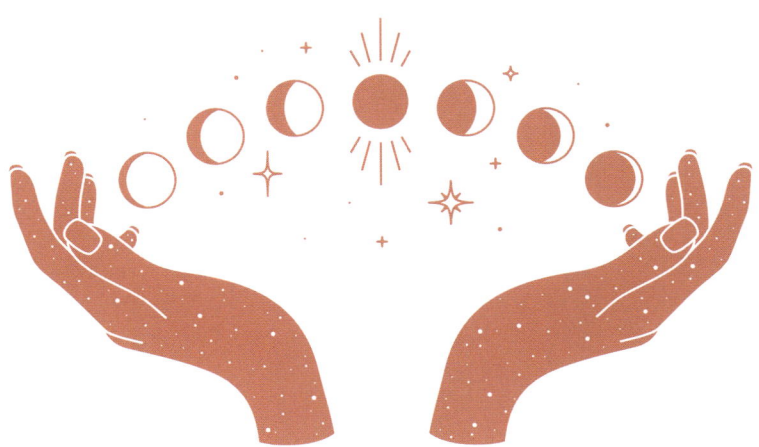

EXERCISE

SHIFT YOUR PERSPECTIVE

Retrogrades are the perfect time to take a step back and look at things from a different viewpoint. This is not always easy to do, but it helps if you get into the habit of shifting your perspective daily. This simple exercise encourages you to maintain a flexible and creative attitude.

WHAT YOU NEED

Some floor space and cushions.

WHEN TO DO IT

Carry this out in the run up to or during a retrograde of any planet, to help you get into the right mindset.

WHAT TO DO

- Lay down somewhere inside – for example, in your living room. Make sure your head is supported by a cushion and you can stretch out and relax properly. You might want to bend your knees slightly so that you don't strain your lower back.

- Breathe deeply and relax.

- Let yourself become accustomed to the view of the ceiling. Take note of everything you can see.

- Now imagine that the ceiling is actually the floor, and vice versa, so you feel as if you are suspended in mid-air, looking at the floor from a different angle. It can take a while to connect with this viewpoint, so be patient.

- Imagine you are suspended, attached to the ceiling by gravity. What would it be like to drop down and walk upon the floor? How would the room look from this perspective?

- Remember, you are tricking your brain with an optical illusion, just as the planets trick us by appearing to go into retrograde motion.

- Breathe and enjoy stretching your imagination in this way, then return to 'normal' (as in, feeling like you're back on the floor) when you are ready.

- Be sure to stretch your limbs and take your time getting up from the floor.

WHAT IS RETROGRADE ENERGY?

Astrologers believe that the position of the planets at the time of your birth help to shape your character, gifting you with certain attributes and strengths. This is because each planet governs a specific sphere of life, and so where it sits in your birth chart has a direct influence on who you become. But it doesn't end there; the daily movements of the planets also shape your individual world, creating energy that can be utilized to enhance your life. When a planet is perceived to be moving backwards into retrograde, it creates a different kind of energy that you can actually feel – as the celestial body retreats, you too will experience a sense of going within, of rewinding time and addressing past issues. In some cases, this reversal of movement can bring about changes and delays, causing you to slow down. In effect, what happens on Earth is a reflection of what is happening to the planet in the sky.

WHAT IT DOES

As expected, this backward movement has a direct effect on you, making it seem hard for you to progress in any area. The energy is unsettling, causing you to question things that you thought were stable and secure. Retrograde energy is confusing, which is no surprise when you consider that what you're experiencing is actually an optical illusion. The planet isn't really moving backwards, it just appears to be. By the same token, you are not really at a standstill, you are being given an opportunity to progress with even more insight at your fingertips. Retrograde energy brings clarity and wisdom, if you're prepared to cut through the illusory veil and dig deeper.

How to prepare for the retrograde motion

Each planet's retrograde is different, depending on the areas they govern, but there are some things you can do that will help you work through any type of retrograde energy. Giving yourself space and time to reflect is top of the list, along with developing a more laid-back attitude to life. Retrogrades can be tricky, so it's important to cut yourself some slack and be kind to yourself and others, who will also be going through their own challenges. Here are some suggestions to help you navigate the journey.

EXERCISE

CLEAR YOUR MIND RITUAL

This ritual will help to restore focus and balance if you feel unsettled during a planet's retrograde.

WHAT YOU NEED

A handful of fresh rosemary (for its association with clarity and focus), a pan of water, a strainer, a teacup or mug, a towel, and a quiet space for reflection.

WHEN TO DO IT

This ritual can be performed at any point during a planet's retrograde.

WHAT TO DO

- Put the rosemary sprigs in a small pan, just cover them with water, and simmer on the hob over a low heat for at least five minutes.
- Once the liquid is bubbling, remove from the heat and strain it through a sieve into a heatproof teacup or mug.
- Take a minute to enjoy the fresh herbal scent of the steam rising from the cup.
- Sit at a table and place the cup in front of you.
- Pop the towel over your head, covering you and the cup, so that you can inhale the steam and feel the full benefits of this soothing herb.
- Close your eyes and draw in a long, deep breath. Feel the aroma settle in your chest, and imagine it pouring through your body, clearing away negative energy.
- Enjoy the freshness of the fragrance as it fills your nostrils.
- As you exhale, imagine you're releasing any clutter from your mind; this includes stress, fear, and worry.
- Imagine feeling this unwanted clutter pouring from your lips with your outward breath.
- Continue to breathe in this way for a couple of minutes, or until you feel relaxed and revived.
- When you're ready, remove the towel and sip the drink slowly. You might want to add a spoonful of honey to sweeten the taste.

EXERCISE

GUIDED MEDITATION

Meditation is an effective tool to calm and balance body and mind in preparation for a planetary retrograde. It brings stability during stressful periods and can help you deal with the erratic energy of a planet seemingly moving backwards. Any type of meditation will help, but it is particularly powerful if you couple deep breathing and focus with a visualization.

PREPARING FOR A
RETROGRADE GUIDED MEDITATION

- This exercise is best carried out a couple of days before the retrograde starts.

- To begin, find somewhere comfortable that you can sit on the floor, if possible, with your legs crossed and your hands placed either side of you. If you find it hard to sit cross-legged, position yourself near a wall so your back is supported, and stretch your legs out in front of you.

- Root yourself by pressing your bottom into the floor and pressing the palms of your hands into the floor.

- Lengthen your spine and imagine a thread attached to the centre of your skull, which tugs lightly upwards, helping to stretch your back.

- Relax and soften your chest.

- Close your eyes and focus on your breathing. Inhale deeply and take your time.

- Picture a space scene before you. You might see this as a giant portrait of the night sky that you are standing in front of. Try to see as much detail as you can in the image, so picture the stars grouped together in their constellations.

- Imagine that you are falling forwards into the picture, gently toppling into the cosmic realm.

- Feel yourself floating in space, in amongst the inky darkness. You are surrounded by twinkling stars and you feel as light as a feather.
- Up ahead you see a planet (this is the planet that is about to go into retrograde movement). Acknowledge its presence and take in its appearance.
- See it gradually begin to move away from you as it reverses. Watch the planet's path through the sky, and simply let the narrative unfold. Don't try to control events, just watch, wait, and breathe.
- If your concentration wavers, bring your attention back to the cosmic vista. Feel the light, bright energy of the stars fill you up.
- Relax and enjoy taking in the scene before you.
- When you are ready to return to the real world, imagine that you are floating backwards, falling back into your head and out of the picture.
- Open your eyes and give your body a stretch.
- Say, 'I release my need to control and go with the flow of retrograde energy.'

DIET

Eating healthy, nourishing meals is essential around and during a retrograde, but this can be hard to do, particularly during Mercury retrograde. The disruptive energy of this particular retrograde affects personal relationships, causing stress and emotional worry, which in turn leads us to reach for sugary treats. Comfort food is a must at this time, but it's important to make healthy choices. Opt for dishes that have a balance of protein, carbs, and vegetables, and avoid processed foods, which will only clog your system, making you feel heavy and blocking the release of much-needed energy.

In magic, each planet is synonymous with different types of foods, so it helps to eat foods associated with the planet that is in retrograde. Here's a quick checklist to inspire you.

	TRY TO EAT....
MERCURY	Nuts and seeds of any sort, fibre-rich foods like oats, bananas, plums, root vegetables – particularly carrots and parsnips – and leafy salad.
VENUS	Figs, dates, avocado, honey, almonds, mango, berries, pomegranate, sweet potato, and also cream cheese.
MARS	Red foods like red peppers, tomatoes, redcurrants, and raspberries, and also basil, garlic, and spices like chilli, cayenne, and black pepper.
JUPITER	Corn, wheat, barley and other whole grains, yellow peppers, lemons, grapefruit, oranges, and pineapple.
SATURN	Lentils, beans, pickles, courgettes, oats, soy, kimchi, and exotic spices.
URANUS	Fish and dairy products – particularly cheese – peanuts, pumpkin flesh and seeds, bananas, saffron, and chamomile.
NEPTUNE	All types of fruit but particularly citrus fruits, kiwi, melons, mango, shellfish, watercress, cabbage, and spinach.

EXERCISE

JOURNAL

Invest in a journal specifically to chart your moods, thoughts, and feelings during each retrograde. This is particularly insightful as it will help you notice the subtle energy differences when each of the planets appear to move backwards. During this period, try to check in at the end of every day and use the journal as a way of reflecting on events and how you feel. Also use this space to reflect on any issues that might arise from your past. Think of it as a workbook, where you can record your innermost feelings and work through them.

TRY THIS!

Imagine that your journal is a guide, a guru that can help you evolve and emerge from this period stronger and more centred by posing the right questions.

At the top of the page, write a series of questions to help you focus:

- 'What is on my mind?'
- 'How do I feel right now?'
- 'Why am I feeling this way?'
- 'What can I do about this?'
- 'Do I need closure with anything from my past?'
- 'What would I like to create for my future?'
- 'What steps do I need to take to do this?'
- Use these questions as prompts to inspire you.

DREAM DIARY

During each planet's retrograde you'll witness a burst of psychic energy and may experience more intuitive insights than normal. This is because your senses are heightened, thanks to this cosmic illusion which encourages you to go inwards. You'll likely feel more emotional, as old issues surface and new challenges arise, and as your subconscious mind takes precedence. You may feel that you're experiencing more dreams than usual, when in truth it's your subconscious that is working overtime and helping you retain the imagery. To help you work through everything, invest in a dream diary, and use it to record any dreams that you can recall. Even if you think you don't dream, keep a notebook by your bed, and when you wake in the night, record any fragments that you can remember. Also make a note of how you feel on waking and any emotions that you recall from your dreams, as these could be important in deciphering their meaning. Finally, note down any recurring symbols or narratives. Recurring dreams are particularly important as they highlight issues that need your attention.

DECODE YOUR DREAMS

Make a point of reading through your dream diary at the end of every week. You may notice a theme developing, or symbols that appear over again which help you make sense of the core message. To simplify things, read each entry and write down one or two words that sum up the dream for you. For example, if you dream you are lost at sea you might write 'lost' and 'vulnerable', then look at the words you have written throughout the week and see if you can find a link to how you're feeling in your day-to-day dealings. Consider, too, the planet in retrograde and the area it governs, as this may shed light on the type of dreams you are having.

EXERCISE

BREATHING

Exercise is important during any planet's retrograde, as it helps to promote a positive attitude and clear your mind. You might not want to work out at this time, as retrograde energy can make you feel sluggish, but getting active will help to ease any frustrations and boost your vitality.

When some planets move into retrograde, they disrupt the natural flow of your universe, causing chaos, and that's when exercise is even more beneficial as it helps you work through your emotions in a safe and healthy way. Mercury and Mars have this effect, stimulating the adrenal glands and causing you to feel unsettled and charged with energy. To combat this, build some sort of exercise into each day, even if it's just a brisk walk to work in the morning, as this will help you stay balanced and calm.

Breathing is a key part of your exercise routine. Ensuring that you breathe fully will flood your body and brain with oxygen, providing much-needed clarity and helping to soothe your mind.

TRY THIS!

- At regular intervals in your day, stop what you are doing and turn your attention to your breathing. How deeply are you inhaling? And how fast?

- Place a hand on the centre of your chest and notice the rise and fall as you breathe.

- Draw a long, deep breath in to the count of four slow beats.

- Hold the breath in your chest for two slow counts, and feel the warmth of the energy beneath the palm of your hand.

- Exhale gradually, letting the breath slip from between your lips to the count of four.

- Repeat this cycle two or three times, then make your breaths even longer by inhaling to the count of five, then holding for three before exhaling for five.

- Do this for at least two minutes, and you will notice that you feel more relaxed, balanced, and energized.

RITUAL

STARGAZING

Tune into the planets and prepare for retrograde energy by doing some stargazing. While you might not be able to see all the planets, taking in the night sky will help you connect with cosmic energy and harness the power of the Universe.

- To begin, you will need to find somewhere that you can sit in comfort and have a clear view of the sky. Hilltops are a great place to set up for a spot of stargazing, but if you haven't got access to this kind of landscape, your back garden or yard will do. As long as you can look up and gaze at the vista, you can connect with astral energy.

- Make sure you have a comfortable chair, with cushions for support and a blanket to keep you warm if it's a chilly night.

- You might also want to take a notebook with you, so that you can record anything you see or write down any thoughts.

- Sit back and relax. Breathe deeply and gaze upwards at the vista. What can you see? At first it will be a blanket of darkness, but as you stare you'll begin to notice clusters of stars, some brighter than others.

- What kind of patterns do you see? Perhaps you'll be able to recognize a constellation, or locate the North Star. Don't worry if you can't pick out anything obvious, just relax and enjoy the view.

- Let your gaze soften and your imagination take over. You might begin to see narratives unfold, just as the Ancients before you made up stories and myths, by looking at the heavens and giving the planets and stars various attributes.

- Imagine that you are able to soar above the clouds, up into the cosmos in amongst the stars. Close your eyes and picture what you might see. Picture your favourite planet, or the planet that governs your zodiac sign. Imagine breathing in the power of this planet.

- Open your eyes and take in the view again, letting it wash over you.

- See the night sky as an enormous blanket wrapped around the Earth. Enjoy your time beneath the stars and let the peaceful atmosphere seep beneath your skin and soothe your soul.

ACTIVITIES TO DO AND AVOID DURING ANY RETROGRADE

Retrogrades are an opportunity to reassess your life and acknowledge how far you have come. Packed with potential, they can help you address issues that may be holding you back, and also make plans for the future. You may realign with your life's purpose, or completely change your attitude and approach based upon events that unfold. The key with this is not to make any hasty decisions. Instead, take some time out and reflect. Be open to the changes, and learn to go with the flow.

THINGS TO AVOID
AT THIS TIME

The unpredictable energy that occurs during a retrograde means that certain activities are best avoided. Here are a few examples of things you should try to refrain from doing.

MAKING KEY DECISIONS

The erratic energy of a retrograde can make you feel vulnerable, and you may want to take some kind of action to restore the balance, but try to hold off. Wait until you have passed through the retrograde and things have settled again. You may find that once everything has calmed down, you don't need to change anything at all. Retrogrades stir up emotions purposely to help you work through issues, but try not to act impulsively. Instead, hit pause, acknowledge any thoughts and feelings that you have, and sit with them for a while. Treat this time as a period of reflection. If at the end of the retrograde you still feel like taking the same action, go ahead, but give yourself time to process everything.

CONFRONTATION OR CONFLICT

The unpredictable energy of a retrograde can ruffle feathers in many ways. Usually-calm individuals may feel instantly on edge or overwhelmed with unsettling emotions like anger, fear, or frustration. It can be hard to know how to deal with these feelings, and the natural impulse is to act on them. While this may help initially, it can cause more problems down the line once retrograde energy has dissipated. Try to resist spontaneous outbursts, instead, take a step back. If you find yourself in a situation where you feel you might explode, count to ten slowly and focus on your breathing. Think about something that makes you feel happy, or recall a fond memory, to switch up your mindset. Channel your emotions into something more productive; for example, you might want to go for a run, take an exercise class, or get stuck into a DIY or garden project. It's also a good idea to write down how you are feeling. Get it all out onto the page, to help you release any negativity. When the retrograde has passed you may still feel aggrieved, and that you want to address these issues, but you will be able to do it in a calmer, less erratic way.

LAUNCHING A NEW PROJECT

Retrogrades are notoriously unpredictable, and depending on the planet that is moving backwards, things can go awry quickly. For example, when Mercury moves into retrograde, communications of all kinds become tricky, contracts are often delayed, travel arrangements can turn on their head, and business activities are plagued with trials. Venus has a similar effect, causing overwhelming emotions to surface. Issues from the past can arise to blight current relationships, including friendships, and financial plans may hit problems. With all of this unstable energy, it's not a good time to launch something new. Wait until the retrograde has passed and instead use this time to evaluate where you are and how far you have come.

GETTING STRESSED ABOUT THE SMALL STUFF

This is easier said than done during any retrograde. The important thing to remember is to look at the bigger picture. Acknowledge that the cosmic climate is going to have an effect on your everyday routine and will cause all sorts of niggles to arise, then cut yourself some slack. Try to engage a sense of humour, and thank the Universe for these mini trials and tribulations. Breathe and go with the flow rather than resisting the changes.

Top Tip

Once you have mastered slow breathing (see page 32), imagine you are breathing in the powerful energy of the planet in retrograde. To help visualize the colour associated with the planet – for example, Mars – imagine that you're drawing in vibrant red energy and exhaling the same. For Venus you might visualize bright pink energy, and for Mercury you might visualize a vivid emerald-green hue.

THINGS TO DO AT THIS TIME

Retrogrades can be precarious times when it comes to decision-making, but they do provide plenty of potential to reflect upon your current situation and evaluate your progress.

SLOW DOWN

Retrograde energy may appear to be chaotic, but what it actually does is cause you to slow the pace of your life and take stock. It provides an opportunity for you to take your foot off the gas and coast along for a while. You may find that you cannot make any real progress in this period, but that's fine. Instead, take your time and connect with the world around you. Don't rush headlong into things. Give every activity some thought, even those everyday things that you normally speed through. Be careful in your thoughts, words, and actions and appreciate each activity and what it brings to your life.

ENGAGE WITH NATURE

Use this period of slowing down to engage with the world around you. Reconnect with nature, and build time in your schedule to get outside and experience the landscape. Go for regular walks in your local park or nature reserve. Get out in the garden and get your hands dirty. Engage all of your senses as you do this, so take in not only what you can see, but also what you hear, smell, taste, and touch. Be present and in the moment and enjoy the experience. You might want to journal about this, or do something creative inspired by your time in nature.

BE COMPASSIONATE

It can be hard to be compassionate when your emotions are fluctuating, but endeavour to be kind. Remember that everyone is going through a similar thing and feelings are heightened at this time. Smile and share some love. Be thoughtful in the things you do, and make a difference by listening and caring. Reach out to friends and family, but also to those people who might be on the fringes of your world. Be good to yourself when you feel low. Instead of letting your inner critic run wild when something doesn't go well, breathe, place a hand on your heart, and say, 'I am enough, this is enough, everything is fine.'

REMAIN OPEN AND FLEXIBLE

Try to remain open to what is happening around you. Be flexible when problems occur and instead of resisting them, go with the flow and work around them. This will reduce the amount of stress you experience. Be adaptable in your approach to others, too, and try not to form or stick to rigid opinions, which can be limiting. For a while change can be confronting but accept that it may work out for the best in the long run. Don't make any hasty judgements, simply let the process unfold. It could be that you're re-aligning to a new way of thinking and being that will benefit you in the future.

REFLECT AND RE-EVALUATE

Use this time to reflect upon your life and the things you have achieved so far. Acknowledge your achievements and give thanks for the positive things in your world. This will help you feel more balanced and confident. Think about what you would like to achieve in the future, and consider the steps you could take to do this. Don't act, simply evaluate where you are and how you might shape the future, and make any notes so that you can look back and have a starting point when the energy shifts once more.

TAKE YOUR TIME COMMUNICATING

Stop and think before you speak. Retrogrades, particularly those in Mercury, affect the way we engage with others, so reflect carefully on what you want to say before opening your mouth. Consider how the other person might react, and take a minute to mull things over. Be sure that what you want to say delivers the right message, and always apply extra care and compassion in the words you choose.

CHAPTER TWO
PLANET PROFILES

Every planet and star within the Solar System is uniquely different. Some are gas giants enveloped in swirling mists and wraithlike rings, while others have ice and rock at their core. Then there's the satellite that is the Moon, which holds a prominent place in the night sky. To the astronomers of old who mainly wrote and spoke Latin, these celestial beauties lit up the heavens and were imbued with powerful magic. No wonder they were named after major gods and goddesses in Roman mythology and seen as physical manifestations of these deities. The astral pantheon had a place and purpose, and was worshipped by those on Earth who took comfort in its nightly presence, and so the narratives grew and qualities were ascribed to each planet which have evolved over time.

Today, we assign a range of properties to these planets, based on this and the astrological sign that they are linked to. Like those ancient mystics, we have learned to work with their specific energy and harness it in a way that can benefit us. Within this chapter you will find an outline of all of the planets, including the Sun and the Moon, as these govern specific astrological signs. There's a brief description of each, highlighting important aspects and looking in depth at attributes and gifts and how you can use them in your daily life. You will find hints, tips, and simple rituals that can be incorporated into your routine and help you tap into the planet's specific energy.

PLANET PROFILE

Mercury

STAR SIGNS	Gemini and Virgo
ELEMENTS	Air
COLOURS	Green and yellow
CRYSTALS	Aventurine and turquoise
HERBS AND PLANTS	Fenugreek and mint
DAY OF THE WEEK	Wednesday

HOW TO THRIVE IN RETROGRADE

The planet of communication, Mercury is by far the smallest in the Solar System and is also the closest to the Sun. As you might expect from a planet named after the swift Roman god of commerce and industry, it has a speedy orbit around the Sun, travelling around 29 miles per second every 88 days.

With changeable temperatures, Mercury is hotter than hot at 427°C (800°F) in the day, but at night plunges to as low as -179°C (-290°F). Thus it cannot sustain life, but its influence on our lives should not be underestimated. Mercury governs how we think and respond in any situation, as it was associated with intellect and the ability to express ideas by the Ancient astronomers, and being linked to the element of air it can be effervescent. People ruled by this planet are usually gregarious and blessed with the ability to think on their feet. They are gifted with creative flair, and how they choose to use this is up to them, but advocates of this planet are likely to be inventive and engaging in the way they communicate. Mercury's association with business means it does have a serious side, and when in retrograde it can pose a number of challenges that affect the progress of every star sign.

Mercury Planet Fact

The Babylonians, who were the first to document this planet's retrograde movements in around the 7th century BCE, associated it with their god of wisdom, Nabu. Known as the 'divine scribe', Nabu's area of influence was, like the god Mercury, linked to writing and communication. Interestingly, many of the craters upon this planet's rocky surface are now named after artists and writers, with one entitled 'Geisel' after Dr. Seuss, whose full name was Theodor Seuss Geisel.

RITUAL

TO HELP YOU CONNECT WITH THE CREATIVE ENERGY OF MERCURY

- Cup a piece of turquoise in both hands.
- Breathe deeply, and imagine you're drawing in the vibrant blue energy of the stone.
- As you breathe out, say, 'I release my creativity and let it flow through me.'
- Continue to breathe in this way for a minute, then relax and let any thoughts or ideas surface in your mind.

TUNE INTO THE ENERGY OF MERCURY WITH THESE DAILY TIPS AND SUGGESTIONS

Mercury is all about engaging with the world around you. Its influence can be felt in your interactions with others, and your environment. Practise the tips below and make them a part of your routine, to help you create and sustain valuable connections that will bring you success and harmony.

- Be mindful in your interactions with others. Listen carefully to what is being said and use your intuition to help you understand any subtle or underlying messages – look for clues in body language and facial expression.

- Take regular walks outside in the fresh air and engage all of your senses as you do this. Think about not only what you can see, but what you can hear, feel, smell, and touch.

- Do something creative every day. This could be something simple like doodling or sketching in a notebook, journalling, or singing along to your favourite song.

- Take a breath. Mercury is associated with the element of air, and breathing slowly and deeply will bring focus and clarity to your communications. Inhale to the count of four, hold the breath for two counts, then exhale to the count of four.

SELF-CARE RITUAL

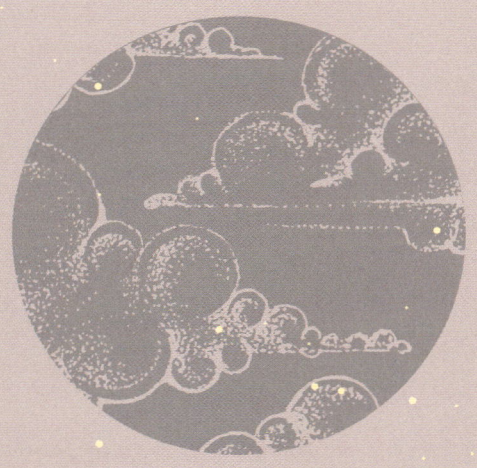

TO HELP YOU EXPRESS YOURSELF
WITH CONFIDENCE AND EASE

WHAT YOU NEED

Some time and space to visualize.

WHEN TO DO IT

Carry out this ritual on a Wednesday, the day most associated with the planet Mercury.

WHAT TO DO

- To begin, find a comfortable place to sit without distractions.
- The throat chakra, which is situated in the centre of the throat, is associated with communication, and the colour blue is linked to the planet Mercury. Close your eyes and bring your attention to the centre of your throat. Imagine a ball of blue energy settling in this area.
- See the ball expanding outwards. Imagine that with every breath it gets bigger and brighter, like a flower with petals of light that stretch in every direction.
- Feel the energy reverberating through your throat.
- Know that, like this flower, you can open up and express yourself fully.
- Open your eyes, then gently stretch your neck.

PLANET PROFILE

Venus

STAR SIGNS	Taurus and Libra
ELEMENTS	Earth and water
COLOURS	Pink, green, and blue
CRYSTALS	Rose quartz and emerald
HERBS AND PLANTS	Catnip, geranium, and rose
DAY OF THE WEEK	Friday

Also known as the 'Morning Star' because it rises in the east, the beautiful planet Venus is synonymous with love and the Roman goddess of the same name. Similar in size to the Earth, it's the second planet from the Sun, with a circular orbit and an average distance from the burning orb of around 67 million miles.

With its influence on relationships, Venus is all about romance and what the heart desires. It shines a light on what we value most, from our nearest and dearest to the more material things we crave. Our passions come to fruition when Venus features in our sign, and those who are ruled by this planet, or find it in a prominent position in their birth chart, will place beauty high on the list. That's not to say that they're superficial in any way, it's more that they appreciate the aesthetic and making things look nice is a way of sharing the love. From frivolous flirtations to the powerful pull of soul mates, Venus plays a part in all matters of the heart, and can help us heal and open up to new connections. This planet also encourages self-expression and can help you find your true passion in life.

Venus Planet Fact

The symbol for Venus is a combination of a circle and a cross, and it's also used as the symbol for 'female'. Scholars believe the shape is a representation of the handheld mirror that was associated with the Roman goddess of the same name. It is also the chemical sign for copper, which was used to make mirrors in ancient times.

RITUAL

TO HELP YOU CONNECT WITH THE LOVING ENERGY OF VENUS

- Spend a couple of minutes gazing at your reflection in the mirror.
- Smile, noticing how it lights up your face.
- See the sparkle in your eyes and all of the wonderful things that make you unique.
- Say the affirmation, 'I am loved' three times, with feeling!

TUNE INTO THE ENERGY OF VENUS EVERY DAY WITH THESE TOP TIPS

The loving energy of this planet is all around us; it's in the little things that bring us joy daily. To help you connect at a deeper level, make a point of practising kindness to yourself and others, and incorporate the following suggestions into your weekly routine.

- Nurture yourself with a pampering treat every day. For example, you might want to take a soak in a scented bubble bath, or cook your favourite nourishing meal from scratch.

- Wear the colours of this planet to harness the feel-good energy. You might want to go for green or blue accessories, or add a touch of pink lip gloss before you leave the house.

- Radiate love by being friendly. Don't save those smiles just for people you know, spread them liberally and smile at everyone that you meet throughout your day.

- Tap into the element of earth, associated with Venus. Take a minute to stand outside and feel this connection. Press your feet into the ground, draw a long, deep breath in, and imagine roots stretching from each sole and anchoring you to the earth.

SELF-CARE RITUAL

**TO BOOST SELF-ESTEEM AND
HELP YOU SHINE YOUR LIGHT**

WHAT YOU NEED

Some time and space to think and a journal.

WHEN TO DO IT

Carry out this ritual on a Friday, the day most associated with the planet Venus.

WHAT TO DO

- Get comfortable, and sit for a moment with your journal. You might want to light a candle and burn some scented oil to create a relaxing atmosphere.
- Bring to mind all of the positive qualities that you have; these could be traits, skills, talents, or characteristics. It can often be hard to think of these things, because we tend to focus on the negative side of our personality, but try to remember all the lovely compliments you have received in the past. If you're struggling, ask a friend to help.
- Make a list of each quality or gift in your journal; for example, you might say, 'I'm a good listener' or 'I can sing'.
- When you have done this, read through all of the things you've listed and take a moment to think about each one. Know that you are unique and perfect as you are.
- At the end of each week, re-read the list and add to it as new qualities and talents arise.

PLANET PROFILE

Mars

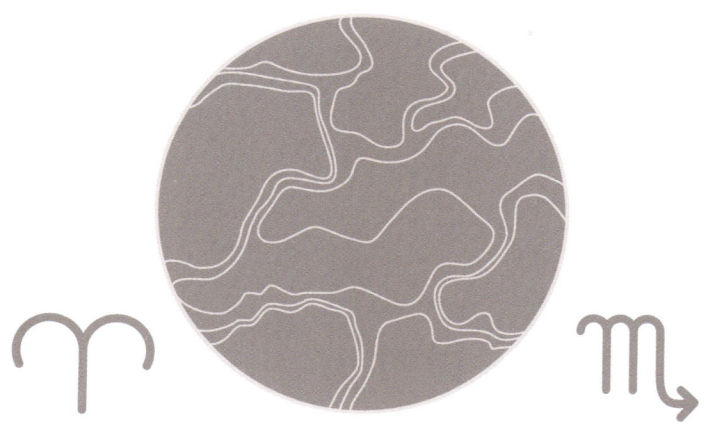

STAR SIGNS	Aries and Scorpio
ELEMENTS	Fire
COLOURS	Red and deep magenta
CRYSTALS	Bloodstone and carnelian
HERBS AND PLANTS	Black pepper and nettle
DAY OF THE WEEK	Tuesday

Known as the Red Planet because of its vibrant hue, Mars is this colour thanks to the amount of iron oxide in its rocky surface. Named after the Roman god of war, it is the fourth planet from the Sun and can be seen from Earth with the naked eye. It may be the second smallest planet in the Solar System, but what it lacks in size it makes up for in dynamism; it is home to the highest mountain, a volcano named Olympus Mons, and has two moons called Phobos and Deimos. It has an egg-shaped orbit of the Sun, which means that while its days are roughly the same length as those here on Earth, the seasons are more extreme.

The scarlet shade of this planet was likely the original reason for its association with battle and bloodshed, but it is a force to be reckoned with and this can be felt in the astrological influence it has on us. Mars is synonymous with action and movement and encourages us to step up and lead when the going gets tough. Like the Roman god of the same name, this is the planet of passion and having the courage of your convictions. Those governed by Mars will be brave of heart and loyal, but may lack patience at times. That said, they have a powerful and reassuring presence and their no-nonsense attitude helps them get ahead of the competition.

Mars Planet Fact

♂ The third month of the year, March is associated with the planet Mars, thanks to the Romans. They paid homage to the god of the same name during this month, because it marked the beginning of their military campaign season. This is also the reason for the month's moniker, which comes from the name of the deity and the planet.

RITUAL

TO HELP YOU CONNECT
WITH THE POWERFUL ENERGY OF MARS

- Stand with your feet hip width apart, shoulders relaxed.
- Draw a long deep breath in, imagining pulling it up from the ground with your hands, up into your chest.
- Exhale sharply, pushing down with your hands and dropping into a semi-squat.
- Feel the energy pulsing within you.

TUNE INTO THE ENERGY OF MARS WITH THESE DAILY TIPS

Mars energy is all about action and movement. It can help you feel motivated and generate positivity. To tune into this invigorating force, go large and push your boundaries. Let the excitement of something new seep into every area of your life with the following suggestions, which can be incorporated into everyday living.

- Get moving. Start the day as you mean to go on, with a short exercise routine. This doesn't have to be anything extreme, a series of simple stretches or a brief jog on the spot will get the energy flowing through your body and set you up for the day.

- Go red. The colour of this planet is deeply motivational and will help you feel confident and positive. Visualize your body swathed in a bright red cloak. See and breathe in the colour. Feel the uplifting energy permeate every pore.

- Stretch your comfort zone by shaking things up. Take a new route to work, visit a different coffee shop, or say hello to a stranger.

- Wind down with a candle. At the end of each day, light a candle, then gaze into the flame and let its gentle movement calm your breathing.

SELF-CARE RITUAL

**TO HELP YOU FEEL
BOLD AND ENERGIZED**

WHAT YOU NEED

Boiling water, nettle tea bag, a teacup or mug, and a pinch of black pepper.

WHEN TO DO IT

Carry out this ritual on a Tuesday, the day most associated with this planet.

WHAT TO DO

- Add hot water to the nettle tea bag in a teacup or mug and let it steep for at least 10 to 15 minutes, so that the mixture has time to infuse and cool down.
- Remove the tea bag, and add a pinch of black pepper to the brew.
- Stir the elixir in the cup, and make sure it is lukewarm to the touch as you will be using it as a hair rinse.
- Tip your head over the sink, then pour the elixir over your head, letting it run through your hair. As you do this, gently massage your scalp.
- The combination of nettle and pepper will stimulate and enrich your hair follicles, while imbuing you with strength and vitality.
- To finish, rinse your hair thoroughly with warm water, to remove all of the nettle infusion.

PLANET PROFILE

Jupiter

STAR SIGNS	Sagittarius
ELEMENTS	Fire
COLOURS	Air
CRYSTALS	Amethyst and lapis lazuli
HERBS AND PLANTS	Sage and frankincense
DAY OF THE WEEK	Thursday

There's a reason why this mighty planet is named after the Roman king of the gods, Jupiter. Being both the oldest planet in the Solar System – formed from the gases left behind by the Sun's formation around 4.5 billion years ago – and the largest planet – having a diameter that is 11 times bigger than the Earth – it commands the sky. This hefty gas giant is the fifth planet from the Sun and has an atmosphere made up of swirling clouds of ammonia and water. It takes roughly 12 years for Jupiter to orbit the Sun, but it rotates at a dynamic speed, meaning its days are only 10 hours long.

Astrologically, Jupiter governs abundance and our ability to take the lead and carve a path to success. It's synonymous with authority and power, and can help us attain our heart's desire if we're willing to put in the effort and extend ourselves. Those whose star sign falls under Jupiter's golden gaze will be willing to stretch the boundaries and go further afield in a quest for fulfilment. These adventurous souls cannot be penned in or controlled, and they will excel in careers where they can travel and explore new ways of living and being. The planet of prosperity, Jupiter encourages us to strive for the best and, like the deity of the same name, aspire to greatness.

Jupiter Planet Fact

♃ The Great Red Spot is one of Jupiter's most famous features. This swirling, orangey-red mass is an area of high pressure and was first noted in the 17th century by the Italian astronomer Giovanni Cassini. Over time, astronomers concluded that this unique feature is in fact a vast storm, which was created by Jupiter's turbulent atmosphere.

RITIAL

TO HELP YOU CONNECT
WITH THE ABUNDANT ENERGY OF JUPITER

- Stand outside on a clear night.
- Press your feet firmly into the ground and look up at the sky.
- Fix your attention on a bright star (it may well be Jupiter, as it can be seen with the naked eye from Earth).
- Open your arms wide and say, 'I give thanks for the flow of abundance in my life.'

TAP INTO THE ENERGY OF JUPITER WITH THESE EVERYDAY TIPS AND SUGGESTIONS

Jupiter represents growth and wisdom and can help us achieve our dreams, but we have to put the work in, too, and this includes being grateful for the blessings that you already have in your life. Tap into the planet's inspiring energy, by opening your mind to new ideas and taking steps towards enlightenment.

- Give thanks for what you already have. At the beginning or end of every day, make a list in your mind or on paper of all the things you're grateful for.

- Burn frankincense-scented oil. The uplifting aroma will help to expand your mind and boost your confidence so that you can strive for the things you really want.

- Daydream. Jupiter encourages the use of your imagination, so take some time out of each day – even if it's just a minute or two – to visualize the kind of future that you want. See yourself happy and successful.

- Read something new. Jupiter is all about expanding the mind, and you can do this by shaking up your reading list. Go for something you wouldn't normally choose; if you're a fiction fan, read some historical non-fiction or a memoir.

SELF-CARE RITUAL

TO HELP YOU BROADEN YOUR HORIZONS
AND MANIFEST THE FUTURE

WHAT YOU NEED

Some time and space to relax, a cushion, and a piece of amethyst.

WHEN TO DO IT

Carry out this ritual on a Thursday, the day most associated with this planet.

WHAT TO DO

- Find a comfortable spot in which you can lie down, and make sure your head is supported by a cushion and you feel relaxed.

- Place the amethyst over the third eye chakra in the middle of your forehead, which is associated with psychic perception. Then close your eyes.

- Picture a soft purple glow behind your eyes, and feel it spreading through your forehead as the powerful energy of amethyst awakens your subconscious.

- Let your imagination take over now and picture something that you would like to achieve. See yourself doing this, and pay attention to how you feel. Really engage with the idea in your mind.

- Say, 'It is as I see', and mean it.

- Open your eyes and remove the stone, then give your body a stretch.

PLANET PROFILE

Saturn

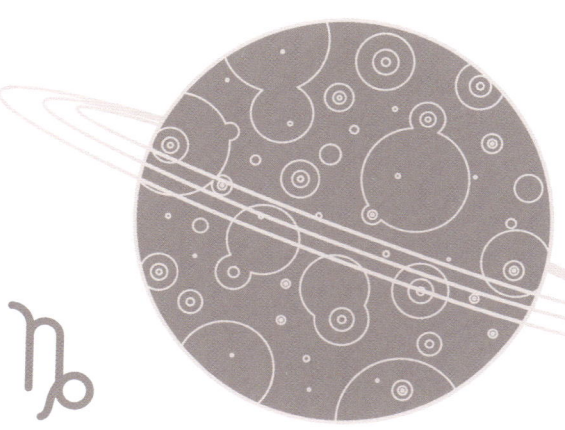

STAR SIGNS	Capricorn
ELEMENTS	Earth
COLOURS	Brown and grey
CRYSTALS	Obsidian and smoky quartz
HERBS AND PLANTS	Solomon's seal and dill
DAY OF THE WEEK	Saturday

This giant ball of helium, hydrogen, and methane is the second largest in the Solar System, and the sixth planet from the Sun. Turning on its axis every 10 hours and 34 minutes, Saturn has the second-shortest day because of this, as well as a low density and fast rotation, making it one of the flattest planets, too. Most intriguing are Saturn's rings, which give it a ghostly aura in the night sky. Made from floating chunks of ice and rock and coated with dust, it's thought that they are remnants of comets, asteroids, and moons that were torn apart in Saturn's powerful magnetic field.

Named after the Roman god of wealth and agriculture, Saturnus, this planet has a sobering influence on our lives. It promotes growth and stability, through hard work and discipline. Saturn teaches us to take responsibility for our own actions, and to step up to the mark. Governing the areas of career and finance, it can help us progress through the ranks. Those ruled by this planet will be hardworking, practical, and resourceful. These individuals like to plan ahead in great detail and are excellent when it comes to organizing themselves, their workload, and others. Setting the rules and adhering to them are what Saturn is all about, and the planet delivers salient life lessons, by throwing the odd curveball every now and then.

Saturn Planet Fact

The Babylonian name for Saturn was Sagush, and the god associated with this planet was called Ninurta. When the Laws of the Universe were stolen by a rebellious dragon, it was Ninurta who retrieved them, making him the ruler of law and order and in charge of the hands of fate. The ancient Greeks associated Saturn with Kronos, the god of time and King of the Titans.

RITUAL

TO HELP YOU CONNECT
WITH THE PROTECTIVE ENERGY OF SATURN

- Close your eyes and take a long, slow breath in.
- As you exhale, imagine your body swathed in a dark grey cloak and see it cover you from head to toe, enclosing you in a protective layer.
- Any negative energy is instantly reflected away from the cloak.

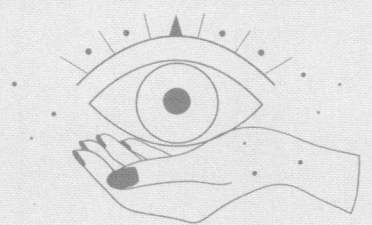

TAP INTO THE ENERGY OF SATURN WITH THESE EVERYDAY TIPS AND SUGGESTIONS

Saturn will help you create order in your life, so that you feel calm and balanced, even in times of turmoil. Its beneficial energy helps you create new growth, particularly in the area of work or finances. Try these top tips to make the most of its powerful influence.

- Centre yourself regularly, by paying attention to how you feel and the way you are breathing. When you're stressed your breath will be shallow, so practise long, deep breaths and place both hands over your heart as you do this.

- Carry a piece of obsidian in your pocket or purse to help you feel balanced and secure. This soothing stone has powerful protective properties and will help to create a sense of order in your life.

- Connect with the earth by planting and sowing seeds. As you do this, let the grains of soil fall through your fingers and imagine that you're sifting through opportunities for new growth.

- Wear earthy shades to help you feel strong, particularly on your feet. This will help you connect with Saturn's grounding energy.

SELF-CARE RITUAL

TO HELP YOU FEEL STABLE, SECURE, AND FOCUSED

WHAT YOU NEED

Some space outside and a selection of stones or pebbles.

WHEN TO DO IT

Carry out this ritual on a Saturday, the day most associated with this planet.

WHAT TO DO

- Create a circle using the stones and pebbles, wide enough for you to sit in.
- Sit in the centre and place both hands on the ground on either side of you.
- Close your eyes and breathe deeply. Feel the support of the earth and the protective layer of the circle you have created.
- Say, 'I am safe, secure, and ready for anything!'

PLANET PROFILE

Uranus

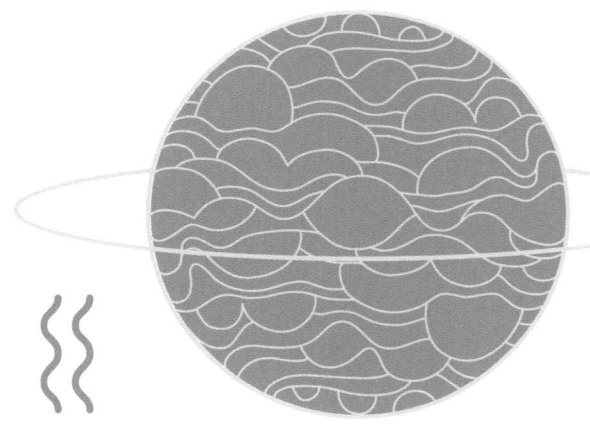

STAR SIGNS	Aquarius
ELEMENTS	Air
COLOURS	Light blue and indigo
CRYSTALS	Amazonite and sodalite
HERBS AND PLANTS	Cinnamon, nutmeg, and mugwort
DAY OF THE WEEK	Wednesday

The only planet to take its name from Greek mythology rather than Roman, Uranus is distinctly different from its celestial brethren, which is no surprise when you consider its quirky and unconventional influence in astrology. Being the coldest planet in the Solar System – temperatures can dip as low as -226°C (-375°F) – Uranus gives off more heat than it absorbs from the Sun and is seventh in line from its rays. It also appears to spin sideways during its orbit. This is thanks to an axial tilt, which puts its equator at a right angle. Scientists believe a collision with an Earth-sized object many thousands of years ago was the cause of this.

Taking its moniker from the Greek god of the sky, Uranus is recognized as the Great Awakener, a planet that can bring chaos and liberation in equal measure. Its influence is revolutionary, and those who fall under its rule are often unique thinkers who aren't afraid to ruffle feathers and instigate change. These freedom-seeking individuals are blessed with an inventive mind and an engaging manner, making them excellent innovators. Uranus urges us to face challenges and expect the unexpected; in doing so we learn about ourselves and the world around us, and often discover latent talents that can turn our life around.

Uranus Planet Fact

Uranus has 27 known moons, and these irregular satellites are made of mostly ice and rock and are connected by one of the planet's rings. Named after characters from the works of William Shakespeare and Alexander Pope, the brightest moon is called Ariel, while the darkest is Umbriel. Other recognizable names include Oberon, Titania, and Prospero.

RITUAL

TO HELP YOU CONNECT TO THE SPONTANEOUS ENERGY OF URANUS

- Stand outside on a windy day with your arms outstretched.
- Spin around and feel the force of the wind buffet you in all directions.
- Come to a standstill and let the breeze swirl around you.
- Say, 'I welcome the unknown and let it carry me onwards.'

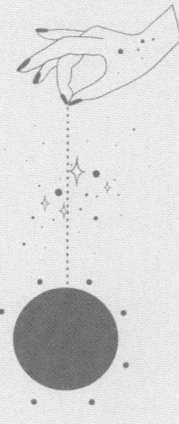

TAP INTO THE ENERGY OF URANUS WITH THESE DAILY TIPS AND SUGGESTIONS

Uranus may bring change and uncertainty, but it also offers the opportunity to grow and learn about ourselves and the world around us. Tap into its life-affirming energy by opening your heart and mind and adopting a positive attitude, come what may!

- Breathe into it. When a situation makes you feel uncomfortable, take a long, deep breath in and imagine it's infused with the energy of this unconventional planet. As you exhale, let go of fear by releasing it along with your outward breath.

- Picture a bright blue light travelling around your body and infusing you with vibrant energy. Imagine it seeping from your pores, to create an aura of vivid blue which attracts new opportunities and adventures.

- The healing energy of amazonite can help you relax in times of stress. Place a small piece beneath your pillow to promote restful sleep.

- When dealing with others, always try to see the bigger picture. Put yourself in other people's shoes and imagine what life looks like through their eyes.

SELF-CARE RITUAL

TO HELP YOU FACE CHANGE AND
EMBRACE THE UNKNOWN

WHAT YOU NEED

Milk, a mug, a pan, and some ground cinnamon and dried nutmeg.

WHEN TO DO IT

Carry out this ritual on a Wednesday, the day most associated with Uranus.

WHAT TO DO

- Add a mugful of milk to a pan on the hob over a medium heat and heat gently for 10 minutes.

- When the milk is hot, pour it into the mug.

- Stir in a teaspoon of ground cinnamon, add a pinch of dried nutmeg, and continue to stir. As you do this, think about the endless cycles of life, which constantly shift and change but continue to flow onwards.

- Make sure the mixture has cooled a little, and sip slowly while contemplating the twists and turns of fate.

- When you have finished, say, 'Change will come and change will go, and I embrace the constant flow.'

PLANET PROFILE

Neptune

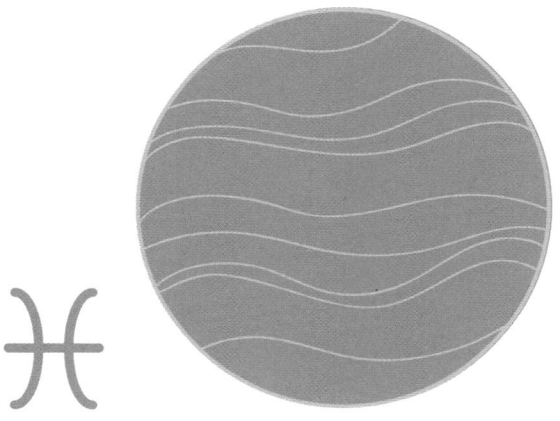

STAR SIGNS	Pisces
ELEMENTS	Water
COLOURS	Violet and deep blue
CRYSTALS	Aquamarine and turquoise
HERBS AND PLANTS	Fern, cypress, and water lily
DAY OF THE WEEK	Friday

The most distant planet in the Solar System and the fourth-largest, Neptune is more than 30 times as far away from the Sun as it is the Earth, making it impossible to see with the naked eye from our planet. This ball of gas and ice has a rocky core, and a force of gravity not unlike that of the Earth, but the freezing atmosphere makes it impossible to sustain life there. Neptune is supremely cold, with temperatures that drop as low as -221°C (-366°F) and gale-force winds that reach up to 2,100km (1,300 miles) an hour. It orbits the Sun at a distance of around 4.5 billion km (2.8 billion miles), and a single orbit takes 165 Earth years to complete.

This planet gets its title from the Roman god of the same name, who originally ruled fresh water. He soon became equated with the Greek god Poseidon, and adopted a new realm – the sea – making Neptune synonymous with the element of water in all its forms. A planet of illusion and imagination, Neptune influences the creative mind and boosts intuition, helping us to see beyond the veil. The dreamy energy of Neptune permeates every aspect of life, and can cause confusion, but it is also deeply inspiring. Those who fall under its glare are sensitive, intuitive souls, prone to mood swings and flights of fancy. Highly artistic, these gentle characters are extremely perceptive.

Neptune Planet Fact

 This planet takes a long time to orbit the zodiac, usually around 165 years, and because of this it spends around 14 years in each star sign. The ethereal influence of Neptune can be seen in its scientific symbol, a glyph of Poseidon's trident and a nod to the realm of the sea.

RITUAL

TO HELP YOU CONNECT WITH THE IMAGINATIVE ENERGY OF NEPTUNE

- Put a little cold water into the sink and dip your fingers in.
- Feel the water flow around your hands, and notice the sensation of the liquid against your skin.
- Remove your hands and sprinkle a few drops of the water on the centre of your scalp.
- Let the cool drops stimulate your subconscious as they trickle over your head.

TAP INTO THE ENERGY OF NEPTUNE WITH THESE EVERYDAY TIPS AND SUGGESTIONS

The transitional energy of this planet helps you delve deep and see beneath the surface. It heightens your sensitivity when experiencing the world around you. Tune in to this power by paying attention to your emotions and staying present as you go about your day.

- Check in with yourself throughout the day. Take a minute to connect with your emotions. How do you really feel? Acknowledge this and be aware of your shifting moods.

- Connect with free-flowing water. It might not be possible to visit the sea, but take the opportunity whenever you can to spend time by water, whether that's a river, lake, or pond, or simply taking a dip in a local swimming pool.

- Repeat this affirmation: 'My emotions ebb and flow to help my intuition grow.'

- Immerse yourself in the colours of this planet. Create a corner dedicated to Neptune and fill it with deep blue and violet cushions and throws and images of the sea, then use it as your relaxing space.

SELF-CARE RITUAL

TO PROMOTE PSYCHIC AWARENESS
AND BOOST YOUR INTUITION

WHAT YOU NEED

A bath and a piece of aquamarine.

WHEN TO DO IT

Carry out this ritual on a Friday, the day most associated with this planet.

WHAT TO DO

- Run yourself a warm bath with your favourite bubble bath or bath lotion.
- Place the aquamarine on the side of the bath, close to where your head will be, and lower yourself into the water.
- Relax and enjoy the feeling of warmth as the water laps at your skin.
- Take a long, deep breath and fully immerse yourself in the water, beneath the surface, if you can. Notice how you are cocooned by the water.
- As you emerge, imagine all of your psychic senses are primed and ready to work for you.
- Hold the aquamarine in both hands as you relax, and keep it with you afterwards as a reminder to tap into your intuition.

PLANET PROFILE

Moon

STAR SIGNS	Cancer
ELEMENTS	Water
COLOURS	White and silver
CRYSTALS	Moonstone and quartz
HERBS AND PLANTS	Mint and clary sage
DAY OF THE WEEK	Monday

HOW TO THRIVE IN RETROGRADE

While the Moon is a satellite and not a planet, it rotates around the Sun and Earth and is recorded as a prominent astrological influence, being synonymous with the zodiac sign Cancer. It is the fifth-largest satellite in the Solar System and was formed around 4.5 billion years ago by a collision between the Earth and a rock the size of Mars. While it appears to be the same size as the Sun, it is around 400 times smaller, but its relative closeness to the Earth affects how we see it.

The word Moon comes from the Old English *mona*. Originally gifted this moniker for its link to the Latin *metri*, which means to measure, it swiftly became associated with a range of predominantly female deities from around the world, one of the most famous being the Roman goddess, Luna. The Moon's influence sits within the subconscious mind, it governs the emotions and how we relate to others, while also offering insights and helping us tap into inner wisdom. Feminine power is highlighted by this satellite, and those governed by it have an innate need to nurture. These creative characters care deeply about others, but they can be extremely sensitive and often need to retreat from the world to maintain peace of mind.

Moon Planet Fact

 We only ever see the near side of the Moon, which is about 60 per cent of its surface. This is because it rotates on an axis at roughly the same time as it orbits the Earth, meaning the dark side of the Moon is always obscured. Reason perhaps for its mystical reputation and the secretive nature of those who fall under its influence.

RITUAL

TO HELP YOU CONNECT WITH THE INTUITIVE ENERGY OF THE MOON

- Stand in front of a window where you can see the Moon clearly.
- Place your hands over your heart and ask the Moon to bless you with insight.
- Gaze up at the luminescent orb and imagine the soft glow bathing you from head to toe.
- Breathe deeply, relax, and let any thoughts and feelings come to you.

TAP INTO THE ENERGY OF THE MOON WITH THESE EVERYDAY TIPS AND SUGGESTIONS

The Moon stirs up emotions and sheds light on deeper issues that might be bothering you. It hones your intuition and reveals insights to help you move forwards and step into your personal power. Tune into this illuminating energy by trusting your instincts.

- Get in sync with the Moon's phases. Spend some time learning about the different phases of the Moon, and take note each night of where it is in its monthly cycle.

- Surround yourself with visual reminders of the Moon. Include Moon images in your home and place of work, to boost your intuition and remind you to seek the bigger picture.

- Sip mint tea. This herbal infusion will soothe your body and mind and help you connect with the power of the Moon.

- Trust your instincts when dealing with others, and go with your gut emotions. If you feel wary, there's probably a good reason for this. Equally, if you feel comfortable with someone, it's likely that you can trust them.

SELF-CARE RITUAL

TO BALANCE AND CALM YOUR EMOTIONS

WHAT YOU NEED

A comfortable place to lie down and a piece of moonstone.

WHEN TO DO IT

Carry out this ritual on a Monday, the day most associated with the Moon.

WHAT TO DO

- Lie down with your legs bent at the knee towards the ceiling and your head supported. Press your lower back into the floor.

- Place the moonstone just above your navel area, and close your eyes.

- Slow your breathing down by focusing on the journey of each breath.

- As you inhale through the nose, follow the breath up into your chest area and hold it there for a few seconds before exhaling slowly through your mouth.

- Let the soothing energy of the stone settle your emotions and soothe your mind, and continue to focus on your breathing as you do this.

PLANET PROFILE

Sun

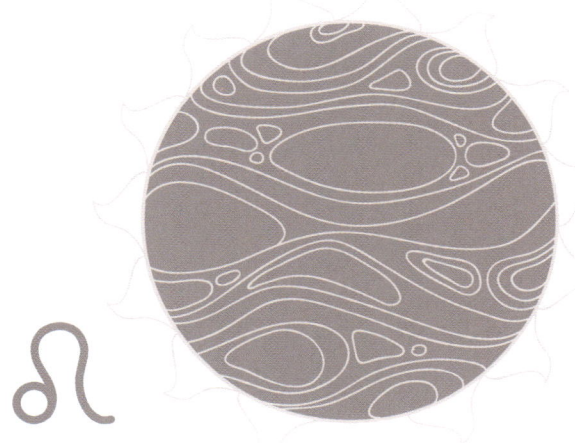

STAR SIGNS	Leo
ELEMENTS	Fire
COLOURS	Gold and orange
CRYSTALS	Sunstone and citrine
HERBS AND PLANTS	Sunflower and chamomile
DAY OF THE WEEK	Sunday

The Sun is the only star that's in our solar system, providing us with light, warmth, and sustenance. It is integral to our survival and takes precedence in the night sky, along with the other planets. A vibrant, yellow dwarf star, this swirling mass of hydrogen and helium has an impact on every area of our lives, holding everything together and in position, from the planets to floating bits of space debris. Its powerful field of gravity draws everything towards its centre. Being 150 million km (93 million miles) from the Earth, it takes eight minutes for its light to reach the surface of our planet – quite a feat for a second-generation star that is 4.7 billion years old.

Astrologically, the Sun represents our core ego and the life force that flows within us. It affects everything we do, and it shapes who we are and how we interact with others. The Sun is the essence of our personality, and working with its primal energy can help us to find our true life purpose. Those who are governed by its influence are natural leaders, able to take control and centre stage. These charming characters enjoy the attention and can be self-absorbed, but they are also extremely generous and loving.

Sun Planet Fact

The ancient Greeks associated the Sun with their handsome god Helios. A radiant being with a halo of bright hair, he would ride his chariot through the sky each day, bringing light and warmth. The Romans replaced the Greek word 'helios' with the Latin 'sol', attributing the fiery ball in the cosmos to the god Sol Invictus.

RITUAL

TO HELP YOU HARNESS THE VIBRANT ENERGY OF THE SUN

- When you get up in the morning, stand in front of a window.
- Throw the curtains back or open the blinds and look out at the view.
- Open your arms wide as if embracing the energy of the Sun.
- Say, 'I absorb your vibrant energy!'
- Pull your arms towards you in a self-hug.

TAP INTO THE ENERGY OF THE SUN WITH THESE EVERYDAY TIPS AND SUGGESTIONS

The life-giving energy of the Sun can be felt in everything we do. It brings light and joy to each day and encourages us to aim high and give our best at all times. Tune into its energizing power with these tips, which focus on creating a positive attitude.

- Get outside. The most important thing you can do to connect with this fiery orb is to stand beneath its rays and let them permeate your being. Make sure you have sunscreen on for protection, then sit and relax in the sunshine.

- Be orange. This shade is imbued with vitality and positive energy. Wear it to lift your mood.

- Sip a chamomile tea while enjoying some sunshine. This relaxing brew will soothe any tension and put you in a positive frame of mind.

- Smile often. A smile is like a ray of sunshine and instantly puts you in a good mood, while spreading joy to others. When you're feeling tense, smile and see how it changes your mindset.

SELF-CARE RITUAL

**TO BOOST CONFIDENCE
AND PROMOTE JOY**

WHAT YOU NEED

A white pillar candle, a pin, and a piece of citrine.

WHEN TO DO IT

Carry out this ritual on a Sunday, the day most associated with the Sun.

WHAT TO DO

- Take the candle and, using a pin, carve a circular sun shape into the wax.
- Place the citrine in front of the candle and light the candle. Watch as the flame steadily grows and flickers.
- Imagine there's a flame in the centre of your chest that grows with every breath you take. Feel its warmth and light fill you up.
- As you do this, visualize yourself cloaked in the Sun's rays.
- Let the candle burn down and retrieve the piece of citrine. Keep it with you as a charm to attract positive energy.

CHAPTER THREE

RETROGRADE PLANETS & YOUR STAR SIGN

Retrograde energy is powerful, and depending on the planet, it can have an effect on different areas of your life. Each planet is associated with specific themes that come to the fore during this perceived reversal of movement, and like any backward motion, this can leave us feeling frustrated.

Mercury is the most potent and frequent retrograde, being closer to the Sun, but the other planets also have an impact. Venus and Mars play an important role depending on where they sit in your chart during a retrograde. Even if you don't know which house they occupy, you can learn how they might affect your star sign and how to navigate any changes.

The outer planets of Jupiter, Saturn, Uranus, and Neptune also play their part in your chart, but their effects are lessened by their distance. Within this chapter you will find a rundown of each planet's retrograde, any useful facts, and information about how to make the energy work for you. Mercury retrograde is covered in more detail in the next chapter because of its power and regularity, but the outlines in this section will help you deal with the other planets as they transition. You'll learn how to make the most of the dynamic and sometimes disruptive energy, so that you can plan ahead for what changes you feel you might want to make, and truly benefit from the cosmic changes.

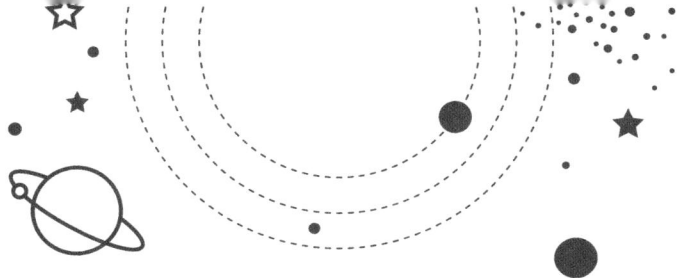

INNER PLANETS

Also known as the Terrestrial Planets, the Inner Planets of Mercury, Venus, Earth, and Mars are positioned closest to the Sun. While they have a much slower spin than the Outer Planets of Jupiter, Saturn, Uranus, and Neptune, they do have a shorter orbit. Unlike the aforementioned gas giants, they are formed from rock and metal and have less moons and no rings.

VENUS RETROGRADE

A Venus retrograde is less common than for the other planets, occurring every 18 months. It usually lasts around 40 days and nights, a fact often referred to in biblical texts. Indeed, some astronomers and historians believe that the Ancients may have taken their inspiration from Venus's 40-day reset, when they used this phrase in the sacred text.

INFLUENCE

This planet's backward spin may only happen every year and a half, but its effects can be felt keenly within personal relationships. Indeed, any kind of relationship may falter at this time, thanks to the starry influence at work. You may find yourself reflecting on past relationships in more detail, examining what went wrong and even trying to reignite the flame. Exes may return out of the blue, and chance encounters could put you face to face with someone important from the past. This is the ideal time to put to bed any wrongdoings and find closure, if you haven't already. Whether you're dealing with a romantic issue or a friendship, you can use this time to make amends by being open and honest, and trying to see the situation from both sides. Making stronger connections with others is what it's all about, and you'll be searching for deeper meaning in all types of relationships, from those with your nearest and dearest to your friends and work colleagues. Don't be surprised if a workplace flirtation transforms into something more passionate under a Venus retrograde. The energy is unpredictable, so expect the unexpected when it comes to love.

Financial matters also come into the spotlight at this time. Venus governs security and self-esteem, and if you use money as a buffer to help you feel good, it's likely that this will be called into question. You could find yourself dealing with a cash challenge or loss that makes you think about your attitude to the material things in life. On a lighter note, beauty regimes may experience a shake up and you could find yourself delving into the world of self-care with renewed enthusiasm, or taking yourself off to a health retreat. Venus prompts you to look at the things you value in life, to decide what's important to you and why, and to take the steps you need to in order to feel and share the love.

Key Words
Harmony, connection, passion, security, love.

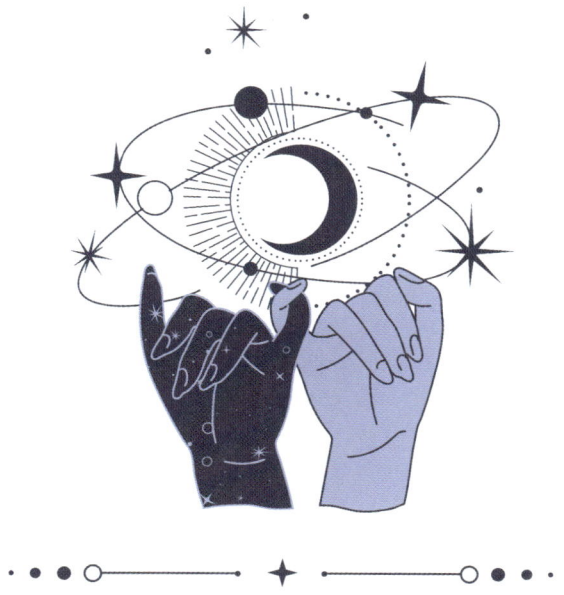

HOW THIS AFFECTS YOUR STAR SIGN

ARIES

You're a sign that likes to progress and you can be impatient, so you will find a Venus retrograde particularly challenging. It may seem like everyone around you is acting strangely, and you may experience some unpredictable behaviour from those close to you, but do not panic, Venus is simply urging you to slow down and think before you speak and act. Be cautious in your dealings with others, and consider their feelings instead of rushing headlong into something with your usual Aries passion. Take a moment to identify your own needs in love and relationships, and make a point of showing your nearest and dearest how you feel. This is the ideal time to slow down and reconnect with the one you love. Do something memorable together, or just enjoy being in their company. Self-care is important during a Venus retrograde, so build activities into your busy schedule that will relax you and lessen the frustration that you might be feeling.

TAURUS

Comfort-loving bulls will feel the need to nest during a Venus retrograde. When things get erratic and unpredictable you seek solace at home, in the bosom of your loved ones. That said, those close to you might be a little more tetchy than normal, and this will upset the status quo. While you'll naturally feel perturbed, try not to let the restless energy of the cosmos get to you. Acknowledge that this is just a blip upon the horizon and an opportunity to work through any past issues that are niggling away at you. As a tolerant Taurus, you often put others' needs before your own, putting up with things when you should really speak out. Now is the time to question why you do this, and to work towards letting go of any resentment or guilt you might feel. The Venus retrograde will make you feel like retreating inwards and indulging, but resist the urge to splurge and instead treat yourself kindly with some pampering to nurture your body and soul.

GEMINI

Quick-thinking Geminis may feel they've lost their usual charm during this Venus backspin. You're usually on the ball when it comes to communicating with others, expressing yourself with ease and winning hearts and minds in the process, however, this retrograde could throw some curveballs your way. You spend a lot of time in your own mind and usually this is an exciting place to be, but you may find yourself pondering past mistakes, particularly in love. You may even run into an old flame, which pulls at your heart strings and fuels a frenzy of thoughts and regrets, causing your usual eloquence to head for the hills. Instead of letting the past pull you down a rabbit hole, relax, breathe, and use this time to take a trip down memory lane, acknowledging the good times and releasing memories of the bad. Get outside into the fresh air and do something physical to get your body moving and clear your head. A stroll, taking in past haunts and celebrating those joyful moments in your life, will stop you dwelling on matters that are now out of your control.

CANCER

Caring crabs may feel more vulnerable than normal and might seek safety under a rock or the nearest preferred refuge, be it the gym, pub, or club. You're a sensitive soul at the best of times, but people don't always see that side of you. Like the creature that features in your sign, you put up a shell (in your case a mask) that you hide behind, but a Venus retrograde leaves you feeling exposed to the elements. Your natural instinct is to smile and carry on with the pretence, but the erratic energy of the stars means you're less likely to get away with it as others begin to notice the changes in you. Instead of throwing yourself into your latest interest or hobby, acknowledge that you're feeling unsettled, sharing your thoughts with those you care about. Express your feelings in a way that is comfortable to you and forge deeper connections with your friends and family. Finances may become an issue at this time, for the crab who likes to keep material things close to hand. Relinquish your hold and use this time to reflect on how far you have come.

LEO

Image-conscious Leos may feel the need to reinvent themselves during a Venus retrograde. After all, it is the planet of beauty that's doing a backward dance through the sky, so it's only natural that you consider your appearance at this time. While you're always conscious of how you appear to others, the unpredictable energy that's around will make you feel awkward and less confident than usual. This is hard for any luscious lion to bear, but it provides an opportunity to go within and examine why you value looks so much. You may start to see things in a different light, and you may even turn away from people or things that you consider superficial. At heart, you're a generous soul and you love the attention of others, but this type of retrograde makes everybody preoccupied, giving you the space to concentrate on yourself in a different way. Self-care and a new health regime may feature, and you could even explore your spirituality. As far as relationships go, you'll address the reasons why you're with someone – are you motivated by what they give you in return, or is there something deeper between you?

VIRGO

Methodical Virgo will feel off kilter during this emotional backward spin. For such a focused sign, you'll be positively out of sorts, unable to concentrate and pay attention to detail like you would normally. This affects your self-esteem, and you'll likely become more self-critical. Instead of berating yourself and others for their shortcomings, take a step back and be kind. Know that everything doesn't have to be perfect and that you can take your foot off the gas from time to time. Use this period to evaluate how far you have come, particularly in one-to-one relationships. If there's a past issue that's affecting your love life, now is the time to address it and find closure. Use your usual practicality to take the steps you need to move forwards, and know that progress comes in all forms. Sometimes doing nothing and sitting with an issue can help you find a resolution in partnerships. Open up with friends and loved ones, and be honest about how you're feeling. You'll feel vulnerable doing so, but it will strengthen those relationships you care about.

LIBRA

Harmony is everything to the level-headed Libra, but a Venus retrograde brings a few bumps in the road. Relationships are so important to you, and you like things to run smoothly in all areas of your life. That said, you can be flamboyant and something of a drama queen when things don't go your way. This type of retrograde stirs things up in a big way, and this time you're not the one kicking off. You may find interactions with others a challenge; people seem more erratic and there is a temptation to take this personally. Now is not the time to challenge them. Instead, use your naturally balanced approach to get to the heart of what is really going on. You're excellent at seeing both sides of an argument, but you may be unusually resentful at this time, especially if you feel you've been treated unjustly. Try not to take things to heart. Socially, it's not the time to mix and mingle, instead, put your energy into making your space a safe haven where you can relax and recharge, then enjoy what you have created.

SCORPIO

Passionate Scorpios will be pulled in all directions during a Venus retrograde. You're intense at the best of times, but while this erratic energy is afoot, you'll feel even more so. Weighted down with past woes, you may long to reignite the spark with an old flame and will likely have the opportunity as fate throws you together, but that doesn't mean it's meant to be. You could also feel the need to throw yourself into new and possibly forbidden entanglements, but while they may be up for grabs, they're not necessarily right for you at this time. You're a ball of energy and you need somewhere to direct this fervour, but resist the urge to jump into anything. Instead, revisit some of the mistakes of your past, remember how you felt at the time and where that led you. Acknowledge the lessons you have learnt, and carry them forward with you. Your mind is restless thanks to this cosmic backspin, but indulging in whims and fancies will only lead to more unrest. Settle your thoughts and emotions by practising self-care techniques like meditation or mindfulness.

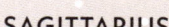

SAGITTARIUS

Freedom-loving archers will feel stifled and will experience a sense of burnout during a Venus retrograde. You're usually proactive, always looking for adventure and pastures new, but the energy at this time will leave you feeling sludgy and listless. Your normal dynamic will shift, and you'll likely be worn out with everything and everyone. Patience isn't at the top of your list of qualities on a good day, but during this backspin you'll be even more snappy and your relationships will inevitably suffer. Don't succumb to your moods. Instead, seek out more gentle activities that will replenish your body and spirit and put you in the right mindset to deal with others. You could even try including your nearest and dearest in your plans, by going out for walks together. Use this as an opportunity to take stock of your one-to-one relationships, to acknowledge the things that are working, and to make a positive change to things that aren't. Resist the urge to expand your horizons at this time and instead revel in the good things you already have in your life.

CAPRICORN

Practical Capricorns will be able to use the Venus backspin to get to the bottom of relationship issues and forge long-lasting bonds. Being a no-nonsense sign, you're not known for your romantic gestures, but this retrograde will make you feel more emotional. While it can be a vulnerable thing to open your heart, you'll want to express how you feel to your nearest and dearest and it's a good time to get anything off your chest that's been bothering you. Secrets are exposed, and problems that you thought were dealt with might rear their head once more. This is not a bad thing; it gives you a chance to examine your motives and resolve issues properly. If a romantic partnership has lost its spark, now is the time to give it a revamp. Go all out to make that special someone feel important by showing them you care in new ways. The bountiful energy of Venus will stir up Capricorn passions and renew your love of life if you're prepared to go with the flow.

AQUARIUS

Quirky Aquarius likes to roll with the punches, but a Venus retrograde brings domestic matters to the fore. You're an inventive soul and you enjoy doing things differently; routines are not necessarily your favourite thing, but it might be worth trying to stick to a schedule during this cosmic phase. One-to-one commitment is likely to be tricky and you may have to go back to basics and rediscover what first drew you to your partner. Friendships are also going to be challenging, and you may experience some unusual behaviour from those you know well. Instead of reacting or trying to solve the world's problems, which is in your nature, take a step back and let things unfold. Use this time to take stock of your life, from clearing the clutter in your home to sorting out finances. You don't normally have time for the nitty gritty everyday details, but this backspin allows you the space you need to tackle these issues.

PISCES

Intuitive Pisces will feel the emotional fallout from a Venus retrograde more than most. You're naturally attuned to the environment and can pick up on subtle changes in atmosphere, so you'll likely sense things before they happen during this cosmic phase. This puts you in a position of power if you don't stick your head in the clouds or get fully drawn into the drama. Your usual dreamy nature may be stifled, and you could find yourself having to deal with practical issues and mishaps. Communication is key during this retrograde, particularly with those you care about. Your inclination to procrastinate and avoid the issue will fall flat and only ruffle more feathers. Instead, try to stay present and in the moment, with simple breathing techniques. Engage your senses and use your keen perception to understand how others might be feeling, and address problems as they arise. It will feel uncomfortable and out of character, but it will help you build strong and lasting relationships.

MARS RETROGRADE

The planet of war might be proactive in nature, but it takes its time going into retrograde, usually occurring every 26 months. This backspin usually lasts between two and three months and is part of a much bigger cycle, which starts and ends the day Mars conjuncts the Sun.

INFLUENCE

Mars rules the ego and is concerned with your inner hero. It encourages you to act and achieve your goals, but when it goes into retrograde you can feel stifled and held back. It might seem like you are taking one step forward and two back, and that you cannot make progress in any area of life. This can be very frustrating, particularly for those governed by the red planet, and this alone can cause all sorts of issues. You may feel tightly wound and find yourself increasingly short-tempered and irritable. Small things will get under your skin during this transit, so it's important to take some time out and find ways to relieve the stress.

Exercise is a must during this transit; it will help you deal with tension and also generate much-needed energy. Being the planet associated with action, Mars affects your general health and vitality, and you'll likely experience a slowing down of sorts. It takes effort to combat this type of cosmic lethargy, so be kind to yourself and understanding of others.

While you'll struggle to make any headway in career goals, this is not necessarily a bad thing, as it gives you time to reflect and consider the direction you're taking. Are you really following your heart? A Mars retrograde calls into question your life's purpose and also what motivates you. It's time to examine the type of person you are. You may find yourself going within and addressing habits and behaviours that no longer serve you. It's not the easiest of retrogrades to navigate, but the Mars backspin provides an opportunity to reinvent yourself, to become the hero in your own story and truly shine.

Keywords
Action, assertiveness, courage, reinvention, transformation.

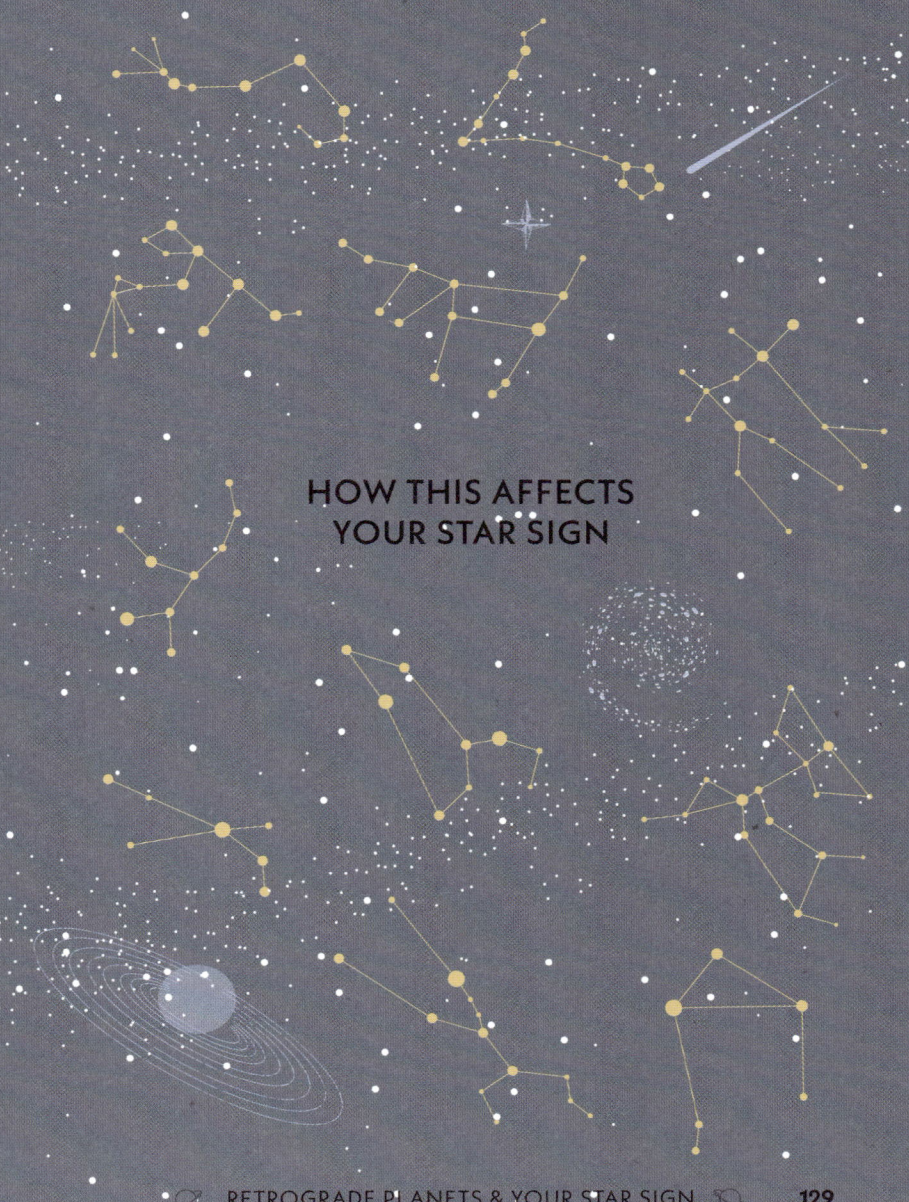

HOW THIS AFFECTS YOUR STAR SIGN

ARIES

Ambitious Aries will need to put the brakes on during a Mars retrograde. You're going to feel the effects of this backspin more than most of the other zodiac signs, as you're governed by the red planet. Normally supercharged and focused on your goal, you'll find your thoughts turning away from career plans and towards matters closer to home. If you do try to make progress with work issues, you'll hit a brick wall or find that you stumble at the first hurdle. From technical issues to competitive colleagues, it's not the best time to try to make your mark. Instead, turn your attention to your nearest and dearest and enjoying their company. Take your foot off the gas and seek fulfilment from your relationships, but also be aware that this starry energy is likely to affect one-to-one communication, causing partners and friends to be more assertive than normal.

TAURUS

Tenacious Taurus has the drive to work through disruptive Mars energy, but they will find the shift in energy tiring. You don't give up easily, and the setbacks that this type of retrograde puts in your path will not deter you. That said, it's a good time to evaluate where you are and what you want to achieve in the future. You can be set in your ways, and this backspin is the ideal time to examine what drives you and why you have certain beliefs and habits – is it down to family conditioning, or your own self-sabotage? The Taurus character loves creature comforts and can retreat into themselves, so exercise is a must. It will keep your energy flowing and help you feel more positive so that you can tackle any personal issues that arise.

GEMINI

As the communicator of the cosmos, you find the Mars retrograde particularly tricky to navigate. You may struggle to get your message across when it counts, and even have issues with the flow of your creativity. This isn't a bad thing; it just means you need to find new and inventive ways to express yourself. You are a mercurial soul, and you live in your head for much of the time, but this erratic Mars energy will get you moving and grooving in the physical world, which in turn benefits your health and outlook. You'll find it hard to start and finish projects at this time, and any progress you do make in your work life will be one step at a time. Be patient and believe in yourself – you will eventually reach your goal.

CANCER

Considerate Cancer goes into battle during the Mars retrograde, but the war is often internal and hard-fought. As you're such a sensitive soul, you can't help but step in when you see others who you care about struggling, but this means that you often get sidetracked. The temptation to turn away from your own path in order to help another will be strong during the red planet's backspin, and this will set you back. You may also find other ways of sabotaging your success at this time. Instead, spend some time in quiet reflection, and consider why you're so keen to sacrifice your own happiness. Be kind and nurture your needs by doing things that bring you joy. Keep long-term goals in mind and don't forget the bigger picture.

LEO

Outgoing Leos crave their moment in the spotlight during a Mars retrograde. While you're always seeking attention, the starry transit shifts this up a gear. You'll be more forceful than ever, and while this might make you feel productive it can put others offside. Don't forget to be kind to the people that give you a helping hand, as you may need them on the other side. Getting your own way will be your main focus and you'll go into overdrive to achieve your goals, but it's important to find some time and space to breathe. Reflect on where you are and how you got there and celebrate your victories with your nearest and dearest. Resist the urge to go full pelt and instead enjoy the fruits of your labours.

VIRGO

Practical Virgos tend to struggle with the uncertainty of a Mars retrograde. You like to know where you stand and you prefer to fill your days with order and routine, so the unpredictable stars will have you in a whirl. Instead of attempting to plough through, use this time to try something new. Turn your mind away from career-focused goals and instead think about how you can do something to make the world a better place. Consider working within a team environment or offering your impressive organizational skills to help others. You'll find the support of team members bolstering and this in turn helps you retain a positive mindset. Practise mindfulness to help you live in the moment, rather than fretting about future plans.

LIBRA

The Libran level-headed charm is often tested during a Mars backspin. You thrive in a harmonious environment, but this retrograde energy is all about stirring things up, particularly on an emotional level. Communications will be challenging, and while you'd normally be able to navigate any awkward moments, you may struggle to smooth things over. Instead of trying to solve every problem, take a step back. Diversify and spread your attention so that you don't become too absorbed in a stressful situation. Go back to your roots with friends and family, and take a stroll down memory lane. Reliving happy memories will help you feel more relaxed and balanced. Know that any tension you're experiencing at this time will fade when Mars goes into forward mode.

SCORPIO

Usually, dynamic Scorpios may experience more setbacks than usual during this cosmic landscape. As Mars is your governing planet, you'll feel the effects of this retrograde keenly. That doesn't mean you can't use them to your advantage; be strong and draw on inner reserves of power. Examine your aspirations and question your motives; this will help to fine-tune your focus, so you'll be ready to make your move when the energy shifts. You're a secretive soul at the best of times, and the Mars backspin could bring up past misdemeanours and events that you'd kept hidden until now. Don't despair! This is for the greater good. You'll discover that finally getting things off your chest, though uncomfortable, can be a healing experience.

SAGITTARIUS

Spontaneous archers feel held back during a Mars retrograde. Like a rocket about to launch, you're primed and ready for action, but nothing seems to be happening. Best-laid plans fall apart, and your dreams of visiting sunnier climes fail to materialize. You're up against the forceful energy of the red planet, and there's nothing you can do. While you might feel restless, try to put that energy into projects closer to home. Take a look at your surroundings. Perhaps it's time to change up your décor, or even think about moving house to somewhere more suitable. Even if your abode isn't on the radar, spend some time with your nearest and dearest, and have some adventures closer to home.

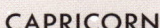

CAPRICORN

Serious Capricorns find it's time to lighten up and unleash their inner party animal during this retrograde. Even if you don't feel like kicking up your heels, it's time to work on your one-to-one partnerships and smooth out any niggling problems. Your methodical nature means you tend to approach relationships in a business-like fashion, but while this organized way of being works in your career, it can alienate friends and loved ones. Sometimes it's better to let your emotions do the talking, and the Mars backspin can help with this. You'll feel more fired up than usual, so use it to your advantage. As your passions surge, so does your ability to speak from the heart. Be bold, take a deep breath, and speak your truth. It could take your personal relationships to a whole new level.

AQUARIUS

Adaptable Aquarians tend to navigate this retrograde better than most, being able to go with the flow. Your flexible nature means you don't let setbacks get you down. You find it easy to see the positive in every twist and turn, and you embrace change with an open mind. That said, a Mars backspin will still have its tricky moments. Social situations could be challenging, as friends and colleagues deal with their own dramas. You may become frustrated with the negative energy, and your usual optimism will waver when faced with a hostile atmosphere, but remember this is only a phase and, like everything, it will pass. Continue to focus on more altruistic concerns, make plans for when the retrograde ends, and use your power for good by helping to motivate others.

PISCES

Imaginative Pisces should use this planetary backward spin to their advantage, by making practical progress with their talents. Your usual dreamy nature means you often feel separated from the world around you, but the forceful energy of Mars will bring you down to Earth quickly. While this can be a shock to the system, it's also the jolt you need to be more proactive, particularly when it comes to your artistic endeavours. Use this time to research, plan, and create. Go back to basics and throw yourself into a new hobby or interest. Doing rather than thinking is the key to working through this cosmic phase, and if you do need some respite, tap into the element of water that governs your sign. Go for a walk along the river, sit by the sea, or simply enjoy a bubble bath and relax.

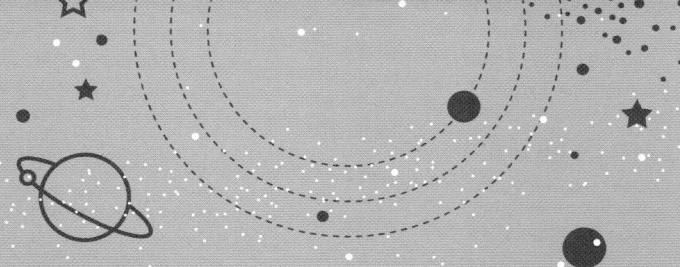

THE OUTER PLANETS

The outer planets, Jupiter, Saturn, Uranus, and Neptune, are also known as 'Jovian' because of their massive size and gaseous nature. This is because Jupiter, the enormous planet that is father of them all, was called 'Jove' by the people of Rome, after the god of the same name – the king of the gods.

These gas giants are further away from Earth, which means they have less of an influence on our lives when they go into retrograde motion. They also tend to go into retrograde less often, but when they do, this period of perceived backward motion lasts longer. Because of this their influence is general, having a similar, subtle effect on all of the zodiac signs. Below you will find a brief rundown of what to expect during each planet's retrograde.

JUPITER RETROGRADE

Jupiter goes into retrograde every nine months or so, and this lasts for approximately four months each time.

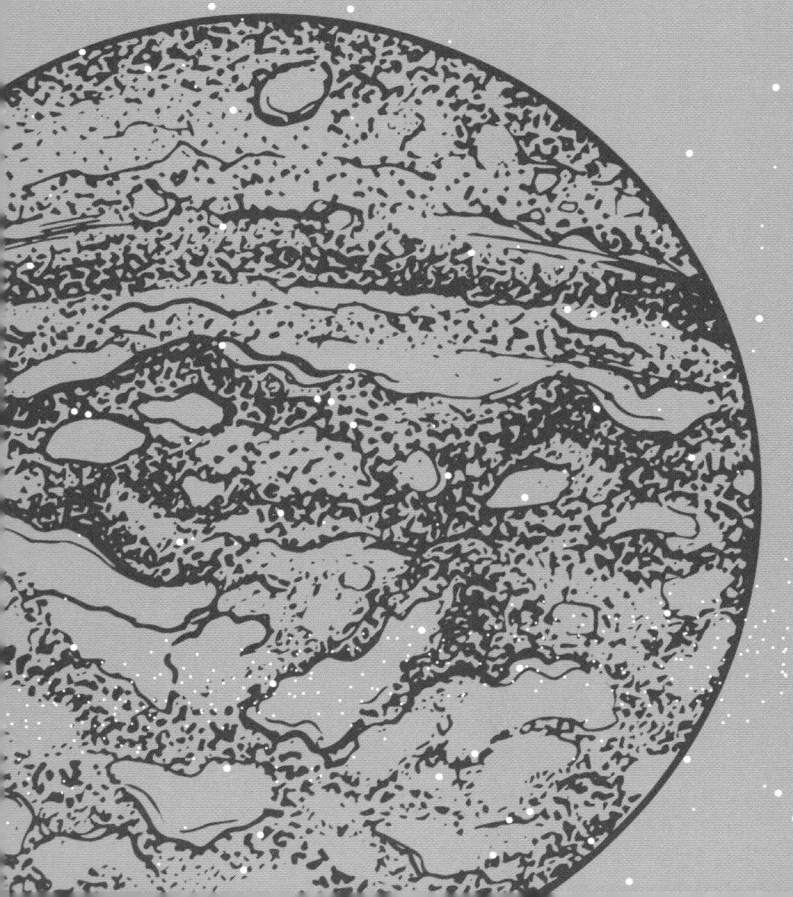

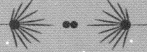

INFLUENCE

Being super-sized, this planet has more of an effect on us than the other outer planets do. Revelations can occur during a Jupiter retrograde; this is, after all, the planet of wisdom and insight, so expect a degree of soul-searching. Long-held beliefs will be challenged, and you'll likely explore the meaning of life and how you can make your mark in the world. Those who have coasted along with little thought about their actions may feel the need to examine their behaviour and make some changes, and the deep thinkers may feel the need to retreat altogether and go off grid for a while. Being associated with growth, Jupiter ignites your aspirations and you'll likely assess and even revise your goals. Anything related to your career will come into the spotlight. Situations that you thought were stable and secure might come into question, but this is not a bad thing. So, your job suddenly seems unstable? Now's the time to retrain and reinvent yourself. Jupiter encourages you to use your intuition alongside logic, to come to a positive conclusion. All in all, this retrograde is about making positive steps towards a brighter future.

Key words
Expansion, introspection, intuition, wisdom, aspiration.

SATURN RETROGRADE

Once a year, 'sober' Saturn goes into retrograde, and this usually lasts for around four and a half months each time, making it a slightly longer retrograde period than that of Jupiter.

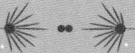

INFLUENCE

The planet of responsibility and authority has a powerful effect when moving forwards. It motivates us to be more methodical and goal-oriented in our approach to work and life. However, when Saturn goes into retrograde the opposite can happen. You may find your focus shifting in a completely new direction. Targets that were once so important to you will have less meaning, and while you'll still move forwards, it will be at a much slower pace. Distractions come from every direction and you could find yourself procrastinating, particularly in a work environment. In the past you might have approached problems logically, but you may find practical solutions are harder to come by. Indeed, you'll need to rethink your entire approach to make any headway, and that's the key during this retrograde. Reflect, revise, and be inventive as you navigate the changes. This is the time to try something new. Don't normally renege control and delegate? Give it a whirl and see if it makes your life easier. Saturn encourages us to press pause on progress, to examine the rules that we normally live by, and to make new ones that are more suitable to our current situation.

Key words
Examination, reflection, focus, inventiveness, progress.

URANUS RETROGRADE

This planet resembles Saturn in its retrograde cycles, which are usually over a year apart and last for around five months at a time.

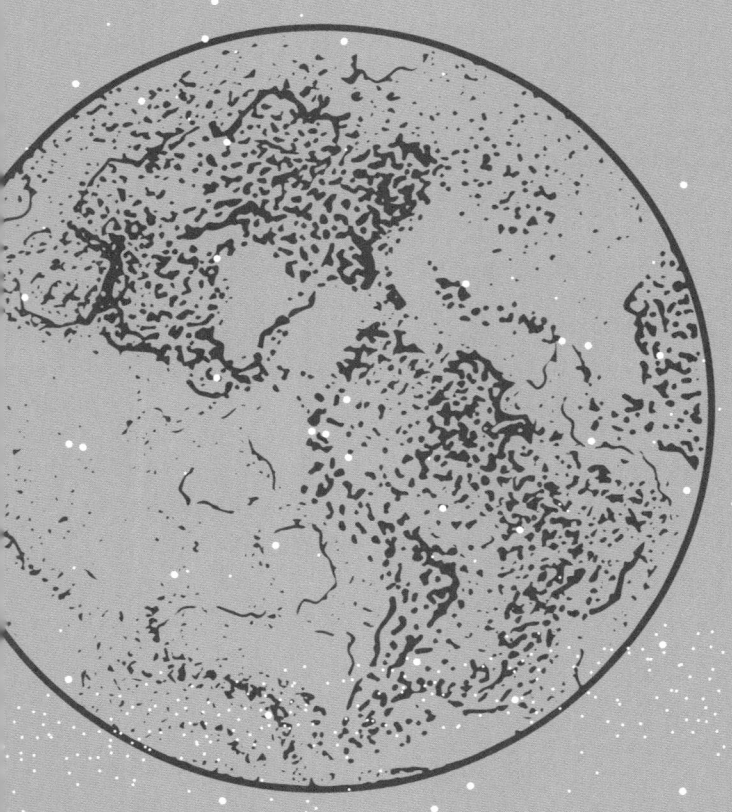

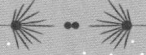

INFLUENCE

It may be slow-moving, but this planet brings revolution and change when it is in forward motion, and it has a similar effect when moving into retrograde. The signs are subtle at first, as Uranus nudges you to explore beyond your comfort zone with the introduction of a new friend or area of interest, but once you take that first step you may experience a cavalcade, as events unfold and you find yourself in new territory. Uranus normally shakes things up on a grand scale, but in retrograde the effects take longer. That said, they'll likely last longer and have a powerful effect on you at some point in the future. There's a gentle encouragement with a Uranus retrograde, to consider new points of view and to expand your world. Plan for that trip that you've always wanted to take, or try that hobby that might turn into a vocation – you never know, it could be a life-changer! This is also the time to follow hunches and trust your intuition. If it feels right, go with it and let the Uranus retrograde lead you into new territory.

Key words
Adventure, exploration, expansion, intuition, action.

NEPTUNE RETROGRADE

Following in the path of Saturn and Uranus, nebulous Neptune has a yearly retrograde which usually lasts around five months.

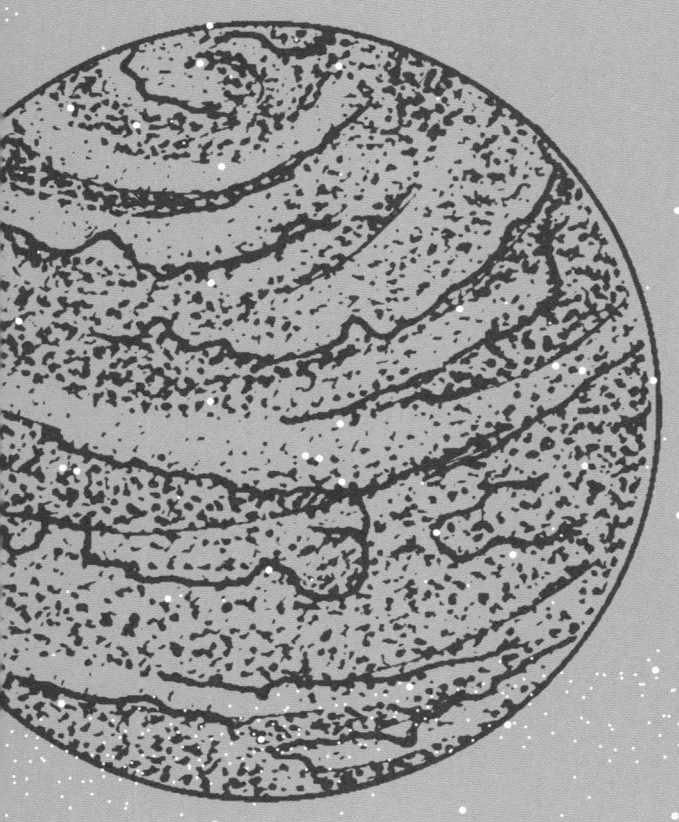

INFLUENCE

The planet of mystery and dreams encourages us to use our imagination and see beyond the veil, by triggering the subconscious mind. Its ethereal influence dances through each birth chart, bringing daydreams and illusions, but when it moves into retrograde the opposite happens. The veil that gave just a glimpse of future secrets drops and all is revealed, so you are faced with a wake-up call of sorts. While the effects are less disruptive than with a Mercury or Venus retrograde, they still encourage you to examine the facts rather than rely on your emotions. Have you been pandering to someone else's whims, believing they had good intentions? You might suddenly catch them out on a lie which ultimately transforms your relationship. Now is not the time to dabble in fantasy; instead, apply logic and get some practical advice on any situation that is bothering you. Check the finer details and let Neptune open your eyes in new ways. Pay attention to the world around you and engage your senses as you explore. In doing so, you'll gain a deeper understanding which will help in any creative pursuits, once Neptune returns to normal.

Key words
Perspective, vision, logic, transformation, understanding.

CHAPTER FOUR
THE RETROGRADES & HOW TO WORK WITH THEM

Mercury is often considered the most important retrograde because its effects are profound in relation to those by other planets, and it occurs more often. During this, and any other planet's backward motion, it's imperative to practise self-care. Whether you crave time and space to breathe, or a little extra love and comfort, it's okay to put yourself first and nurture such needs at these times.

Each planet has a unique energy and influence, so it's important to tailor your self-care plan accordingly. Mercury, being supremely potent, affects each zodiac sign differently. In this chapter you will find hints, tips, and rituals geared to the astrological signs to help you navigate a Mercury retrograde. You will also find a selection of self-care suggestions and rituals to help you work through each of the other planets' retrogrades, so you will emerge feeling better, brighter, and ready to shine.

Whether you want to retreat, reflect, or revamp your life, these tips and rituals are a starting point and will help you to embrace planet power.

MERCURY RETROGRADE

The 'swift' planet, as it is called, Mercury only takes 88 days to orbit the Sun. This means it overtakes the Earth at least three or four times a year, causing a retrograde motion. This period of supposed backward movement lasts around three weeks, making it the shortest retrograde of all the planets. Often a Mercury retrograde will coincide with a transition, which is when the Sun, Earth, and Mercury all line up with each other. When viewed from the Earth at this time, Mercury appears as a minuscule black disc moving across the Sun.

INFLUENCE

Much has been said about the disruptive energy of a Mercury retrograde around the world. Astrologers cite this apparent backspin as the reason for many woes, but while the chaotic energy of this planetary motion can have an effect on all areas of life, it can ultimately be beneficial. Mercury is closest to the Sun, which means this retrograde energy is amplified and affects every zodiac sign equally, although some signs feel it more keenly if the planet is moving through their sign at the time of reversal.

Mercury is the planet of communication and technology, and it steps into trickster mode during a retrograde, blighting any kind of interaction. Emails go awry, letters and parcels fail to reach their destination, and one-to-one conversation can be troublesome, to say the least. Misunderstandings are par for the course during this planetary phase, so be careful what you say and how you say it. Words are easily misconstrued, and you could find that someone gets the wrong end of the stick, and runs with it!

Travel is also a problem area at this time, as Mercury governs journeys of any sort, so be sure to check details and have a plan B, as you could find your voyage, however small, is delayed. Getting from A to B may be an issue in all things and you're likely to see setbacks in personal and business plans, too. While this may be frustrating, it actually allows you to set some time aside so that you can assess where you are and where you're going.

Technology could also hit some hurdles. You may find that your laptop suddenly stops working at a crucial point in your day, or you lose that important document you've been working on for ages. As annoying as this is, try to take a step back and see the bigger picture. Yes, things are not working out as you'd planned, but perhaps you need a break from what you're working on, or you need to rethink your approach? At this time, get into the habit of backing up all your work and take time and care when using technology of any sort.

Mercury urges us to slow down and go within; to use the time we have to get to know ourselves. Talking to others may be tricky, but talking to yourself is where it's at during this backspin. As energy spins inward, so too will your thoughts, and you'll develop a dialogue with your innermost desires and feelings. As strange as this sounds, this kind of communication is essential for personal growth and can set you on a new and exciting path to fulfilment. The good news is that this retrograde doesn't last long, so whatever you do experience, it is only temporary. The most effective way to navigate this period is by going with the flow and trusting that the Universe has your best interests at heart.

HOW THIS AFFECTS YOUR STAR SIGN

ARIES

Strong and assertive, getting ahead in life and love is what drives the focused Aries Ram, and so the Mercury retrograde is particularly tricky for this group. Frustrations arise when things don't go to plan, and you'll have to watch that famous temper of yours. Small irritations could get blown up into much bigger problems, and your closest relationships could suffer. That said, once you've acclimatized to the erratic energy, you'll begin to calm down and may actually enjoy a spot of soul searching. Going within is key. If you can learn to slow down, you'll discover the benefits of stillness to body, mind, and soul.

SELF-CARE SUGGESTIONS

- Listen to some relaxing music to calm and quieten your busy mind.
- Write down your worries. If you're feeling frustrated, get things off your chest by journalling.
- Explore a new hobby or interest; this will keep you active and engaged without causing any stress.

RETROGRADE RITUAL

WHAT YOU NEED

A white candle, candle holder, and a pin.

WHAT TO DO

- Take the candle and, using a pin, carve a circle in the wax to represent the planet Mercury. The circle symbol is also associated with the ongoing cycles of life and is synonymous with strength.
- Light the candle and position it where you can see it comfortably.
- Sit and gaze at the flame.
- Watch as it steadily grows. See it dance and flicker, and simply focus on each movement.
- If your mind begins to wander and you start to feel anxious or frustrated, bring your attention back to the flame.
- Let the candle burn down and enjoy this moment of stillness.

TAURUS

The Mercury retrograde throws light on everything you value, Taurus. From assets and finances to the people in your life that you treasure, you'll feel you're losing your grip on it all, but the reality is, nothing has changed. There may be a few communication hiccups but you're just feeling more insecure than usual, thanks to the starry changes. Instead of wallowing in your perceived vulnerability, use this time to open up about what really matters. Speak from the heart and share your fears with those you care about. You'll find this strengthens the bonds and relieves any tension you're feeling.

SELF-CARE SUGGESTIONS

- Nurture yourself by eating well. Food is a comfort to you, so indulge your inner chef and cook up a storm.
- Get organized. Use this time to clear out any clutter.
- Run a sensual scented bath and enjoy a long soak.

RETROGRADE RITUAL

WHAT YOU NEED

A vase of your favourite flowers, a notebook and pen.

WHAT TO DO

- Sit and gaze at the vase of flowers.
- Connect with their natural beauty by engaging your senses. Consider not only what they look like, but also how they smell, what each flowerhead feels like, and what emotions they spark in you.
- Write a few sentences about the flowers – you can do this as a poem, a narrative, or just a description.
- Connecting with nature in this way helps you see the beauty in the world around you and lifts your spirits during this tricky period.

GEMINI

Gregarious Geminis will be less enamoured with the reversal of their governing planet, which leaves them lost for words. Being articulate is one of your gifts, and you find it disconcerting when you can't express how you feel. Couple this with the growing suspicion that everyone is talking about you, and it makes for a tense time. Don't let irritability get the better of you. Instead, throw your energy into physical activity, as this will help you release stress and boost general lethargy. Even better if you can mix movement with action by doing something productive like a spot of gardening, or DIY, but take your time to avoid any mishaps along the way.

SELF-CARE SUGGESTIONS

- Breathe properly. Take long, deep breaths through the nose and gently release the breath through your lips.
- Get arty. If you're struggling with words, try your hand at drawing or painting.
- Have a massage to release tension.

RETROGRADE RITUAL

WHAT YOU NEED

Some space outside, like a garden or yard, and a small bowl filled with bird seed.

WHAT TO DO

- Find a spot to stand, place the bowl on the ground, and scoop up a handful of seeds. The seeds represent any worries, fears, or negativity that you're holding on to at this time.
- Gently spin around in a clockwise motion, releasing the seeds into the air so that they scatter in every direction.
- Repeat this activity, this time spinning in an anticlockwise direction, to represent the backward motion of Mercury in retrograde.
- When you have finished, say, 'I release my fears, and flow with retrograde energy!'

CANCER

Considerate crabs may find this retrograde tries their patience in more ways than one. You care deeply about others and hate to see those close to you struggling, but it's not so easy to help when dealing with the erratic energy of this backspin. You'll try your best, but you will hit roadblocks at every turn. From running late to feeling depleted, it's likely you'll be frustrated at your own ineffectiveness. Instead of berating yourself, focus on doing things that soothe your soul. Take a yoga class or go for a crystal healing session. If you don't feel like leaving home, curl up with a good book and enjoy some well-deserved downtime.

SELF-CARE SUGGESTIONS

- Disconnect from technology. Switch off phones, laptops, and the TV for a few hours before bed.
- Drink plenty of water, and imagine it's cleansing your body of any stress.
- Massage lavender essential oil into your wrists and breathe in the relaxing aroma.

RETROGRADE RITUAL

WHAT YOU NEED

A dark-coloured bowl and room-temperature water.

WHAT TO DO

- Half-fill the bowl with water and place it in front of you. You're going to scry for insight during this planetary transit.

- Gaze into the watery depths. Let your eyes soften, then breathe deeply so that you feel relaxed.

- Let thoughts flow through your mind while you continue to focus on the surface of the water. What do you see? Do any shapes, patterns, or words spring to mind?

- Don't worry if nothing happens, this exercise is about relaxing and clearing the mind at this time.

LEO

The Mercury backspin reignites the infamous Leo passion for something or someone. While this is exciting, it can make some lions feel vulnerable. You're an all-or-nothing kind of person, and when something comes along that piques your interest, it soon becomes the centre of your world. You could find an ex-love returning, or a hobby from the past could re-surface and steal your heart. While it's easy to be swept off your feet, try to stay grounded. Keep some perspective and take things one step at a time. It doesn't mean that you can't follow your heart, just do so with caution and be sure not to lose yourself in the process.

SELF-CARE SUGGESTIONS

- Count to three before making any decisions or jumping into anything.
- Stay grounded by spending time outdoors – potter in the garden or go for a stroll in your local park.
- Release tension with your favourite workout routine.

RETROGRADE RITUAL

WHAT YOU NEED

Paper, a pen, a small fireproof bowl, and some matches.

WHAT TO DO

- Write down a few words on the paper to sum up any worries or fears you may have at this time.
- Take the piece of paper, roll it up into a ball, then toss it into the bowl. Take a match and light it.
- Watch as it burns to ash. Say, 'I release the past, any fear and pain. I let the cosmic energy restore me again!'
- Dispose of the ashes and repeat the affirmation.

VIRGO

Mercury sends this mutable Earth sign into a spin during its retrograde. You are detail-orientated and precise in everything you do, but the erratic energy of this backspin makes it hard for you to maintain your usual standards. Communications go awry and you may feel like you're not on top of your game. Being critical of yourself and others comes naturally, and you'll be even more so at this time, so watch your step. Instead of snapping, take a breath and connect with your heart. Use loving affirmations to put you in a positive frame of mind, and cut yourself some slack.

SELF-CARE SUGGESTIONS

- When things go wrong or you feel frustrated, repeat the affirmation, 'I am enough, this is enough, all is well.'
- Have some fun. Take some time out to do something you enjoy.
- Be still, take five minutes in your day to sit in silence and breathe.

RETROGRADE RITUAL

WHAT YOU NEED
Sage essential oil and a small bowl of steaming water.

WHAT TO DO

- Add three to six drops of sage essential oil to the bowl of water and position it centrally in your living space.
- Sit close by and inhale the refreshing aroma.
- Close your eyes as you do this, and place both hands over your heart. Feel the comforting warmth beneath your palms.
- Imagine you're breathing in revitalizing energy and breathing out any tension or frustration.
- Take longer, deeper breaths and enjoy this moment of reprieve.

LIBRA

The Mercury retrograde affects the way Librans connect with others, making it hard for them to maintain their usual equilibrium. You like things to go smoothly, particularly with others. You hate any kind of imbalance and have an acute awareness of how people are feeling, so this backspin is difficult to navigate. Speaking from the heart is key, and also taking the time to think about how your words are perceived. Double-check all of your communications, from emails and texts to telephone conversations, before you press send, as things can be easily misconstrued. Try not to take it personally if your usual Libran charm falls flat; instead, go with the flow and let any unease go.

SELF-CARE SUGGESTIONS

- De-stress by pampering yourself; from beauty treats to a soothing soak in the bath, take the time to recharge.
- Dance to your favourite song; getting lost in the beat will lift your spirits.
- Practise visualization, and see yourself in a calm and beautiful environment of your choice.

RETROGRADE RITUAL

WHAT YOU NEED

A selection of tea lights and some space to sit and relax.

WHAT TO DO

- Arrange the tea lights safely in a wide circle, big enough for you to be able to sit at the centre.
- Light each of the tea lights and take up a comfortable position in the middle.
- Visualize a dome of white light surrounding you. Know that you are safe and protected within this space.
- Take a long breath in, then as you breathe out, release any tension with the breath.
- Say, 'I radiate loving energy at this time. I go with the flow.'
- Relax in the space and enjoy this moment of stillness.

SCORPIO

Passionate Scorpios must learn to retrain their focus during a Mercury retrograde. You're usually set on your goal, but this type of backspin creates lethargy and disinterest for your sign. Remember what's important and don't get sidetracked by petty arguments. There will be delays to your already busy schedule, but the key to dealing with these niggles is flexibility, something you're not normally known for. Remember that this phase will pass. Visualize where you want to be and let this inspire you to keep moving forwards. When you hit a hurdle, navigate around it. Personal relationships could provide revelations, and you may unearth secrets from the past, but try not to dwell on them.

SELF-CARE SUGGESTIONS

- Write a daily list of goals and tick them off as you go, to feel a sense of achievement.
- Improve your general flexibility by doing some simple stretches in the morning to set you up for the day ahead.
- Repeat the mantra 'all is well' when you feel stressed.

RETROGRADE RITUAL

WHAT YOU NEED

A piece of clear quartz crystal, which promotes positive energy, and a shower.

WHAT TO DO

- Place the quartz crystal on your shower rack, so that it is near you.
- Turn on the shower and lower the temperature so that the water is fresh and cooling.
- Stand beneath the flow and close your eyes.
- As the water hits the top of your head, imagine you are bathed in cleansing white light, which travels through your body.
- Feel the flow releasing stagnant energy and helping you to let go of any frustrations at this time.
- When you've finished, keep the quartz with you to infuse you with vitality throughout the day.

SAGITTARIUS

Sagittarians usually have the travel bug, but this is not the time to embark on a new journey. You like to be on the move, and while your world view is expansive, this retrograde will dampen your adventurous streak. The starry set-up encourages you to turn inwards and reflect on where you have been, and what you truly want from life. Big questions could feature in your mind and you may find yourself in a sombre mood. Try not to worry too much about this dip in energy. Use it to your advantage and go on a different kind of journey, one that involves soul searching and spiritual enlightenment.

SELF-CARE SUGGESTIONS

- Sit in silence and simply breathe in light and love.
- Invest in a pack of Oracle cards – these picture cards, which can be any theme, are used to tap into your intuition and receive psychic insights. Draw one every day to help you tap into inner wisdom.
- Try a guided meditation podcast, or if you want to get out and about, join a meditation class.

RETROGRADE RITUAL

WHAT YOU NEED

Access to a local park or nature reserve and some time to relax.

WHAT TO DO

- Take a stroll through your local park or nature reserve and find a tree that you like the look of.
- Either stand with your back leaning against the trunk or sit beneath it, propped up against it.
- Close your eyes and breathe in the power and presence of this timeless sentinel.
- Imagine all of the things it has seen over the years, all of the changes that it has experienced.
- Say this affirmation, 'The power of nature flows through me right now,' as you enjoy connecting with the tree.

CAPRICORN

Cautious Capricorns may find it hard to plan during a Mercury retrograde. Your methodical ways always put you ahead of the game, particularly in a work environment, but during this backspin you'll hit delays. Instead of forcing matters, take a backward step. Trust that the Universe has your best interests at heart and that you are where you need to be at this moment. Now is the time to let down your guard, particularly in one-to-one relationships. Open up and let others in. Friendships, too, will benefit from a more relaxed approach and you could find that you make new acquaintances who become significant in your life.

SELF-CARE SUGGESTIONS

- Experience the joy of your childhood and revisit some of your favourite pastimes and hobbies.
- Enjoy being with friends and family; from phone calls, meet-ups, and larger get-togethers, this is the time to reconnect.
- Volunteer within your local community, or help out a neighbour.

RETROGRADE RITUAL

WHAT YOU NEED

Some time to sit in reflection, and a notebook and pen.

WHAT TO DO

- Recall a happy memory from your past and run through it in your mind.
- Engage all of your senses and relive those joyful emotions.
- Now take some time to recreate the memory by writing about it. If you find it hard to put pen to paper, think of a few words or sentences to sum up what happened and how you felt at the time.
- Be creative and connect those words so that you have a poem or a piece of descriptive writing.
- Enjoy using your imagination, and have fun – it will help to open your heart and make you feel more relaxed.

AQUARIUS

Luckily, adaptive Aquarians tend to come out of the Mercury retrograde unscathed. Your flexible nature means you see obstacles as challenges and your inventive mind is always on the lookout for new ways of being and doing, so you'll be able to navigate the changes easily. The only sticking point is your love for technology, which could falter during this backspin. When your go-to gadgets fail, take a deep breath and use your expansive vision to come up with a different plan. Relationships may hit a few sticking points, but your ability to see the bigger picture will help you see things from both sides.

SELF-CARE SUGGESTIONS

- Disconnect from technology, particularly before bedtime, to de-stress.
- Go running; whether you venture outside to clear your head or do some on-the-spot running indoors, it will help to boost energy levels.
- Stay centred by being mindful in your interactions with others and the world around you.

RETROGRADE RITUAL

WHAT YOU NEED

A piece of amethyst and a place to lie down, with a pillow for head support.

WHAT TO DO

- Lie down and place the amethyst over the middle of your forehead. This stone is associated with psychic perception and will help you navigate the retrograde intuitively.

- Close your eyes and take a long, deep breath in. As you do this, visualize a purple flower bud in the centre of your forehead where your third eye chakra resides.

- Imagine that as you exhale the petals slowly begin to unfurl.

- Continue to breathe deeply until all of the petals are open and the flower is in bloom.

- Relax and let any thoughts or impressions come to you.

PISCES

Intuitive Pisces feels especially out of sorts during a Mercury retrograde; being an especially sensitive soul, your psychic impressions are usually spot on, but the erratic energy of this backspin messes with your brain. Others often seek out your advice, but you'll be hard pushed to help with your instincts off kilter. Try not to fret about this change in energy. Instead, use your creative abilities to take your mind off things. You've always been one to escape into your imagination, but while this might not be easy right now, you can still flex those muscles with a guided meditation to help you feel at peace.

SELF-CARE SUGGESTIONS

- Soothe your mind with a trip to the sea, or if you can't venture that far, visit a river or stream and breathe in the peace.
- Carry a piece of moonstone to balance your emotions.
- Give hugs freely, you'll benefit from the warmth of touch and feel comforted by this.

RETROGRADE RITUAL

WHAT YOU NEED

Somewhere to sit outside, a blanket, and a notebook and pen.

WHAT TO DO

- Wrap up warm on a clear evening and find a spot to sit outside where you have a good view of the sky.
- Breathe deeply and take in the vista.
- Look at the stars, and pick out the brightest.
- Create patterns in your mind and see what shapes you can see.
- Let your imagination take over and make up stories and names for each one.
- If you feel inspired, write something in your notebook.
- Enjoy the stillness and beauty of the night sky and let it infuse you with calm.

THE OTHER PLANETS

While Mercury, as explained earlier, is the most important and impactful retrograde, the other planets also have some effects on us when in retrograde. So, to help you navigate all of these, here is a selection of self-care tips and rituals related to each of the planets. Use the suggestions as a starting point and experiment to find out what works for you. The rituals can be adapted to suit your needs. If something doesn't feel right, add your own twist to the mix. Retrograde energy is personal, and its influence can be felt in many different ways. Over time you will learn how to make the most of each planetary backspin for your own individual benefit. You can use these rituals at any time during each planet's retrograde.

VENUS

When in Venus retrograde, it's especially important to focus on self-reflection and self-care. Be open to a deep dive into your heart and use the retrograde ritual to bring calm to your body, mind, and soul.

SELF-CARE SUGGESTIONS

- Enhance your inner beauty by doing things that feed your soul. For example, enjoy a leisurely stroll in the countryside and connect with the glorious surroundings, or treat yourself to a bunch of your favourite blooms and appreciate their beauty.
- Give and receive love freely. Be open and warm in your interactions with others. Hug regularly, and if you have pets, spend some time enjoying cuddles with them.
- Think pink. This is the colour most associated with both Venus the planet and the goddess and it's also imbued with loving vibes, so immerse yourself in rosy shades, from the clothes you wear to your décor. Snuggle up in a pink fluffy blanket and enjoy the peace.

RETROGRADE RITUAL

WHAT YOU NEED

A handful of rose petals, a pan and some water, some lavender essential oil, and a clean spray bottle.

WHAT TO DO

- Steep the rose petals in a pan of hot water on the hob over a gentle heat for at least five minutes. Let them simmer slowly as you visualize what love means to you. Think about what makes you feel safe and happy, and bring to mind any special memories which embody this emotion.

- When you're ready, strain the steaming water into a small bowl.

- Add four or five drops of lavender essential oil and stir gently.

- Breathe in the sweet-scented aroma as the liquid cools and let it calm your mind.

- Decant the liquid into a spray bottle and spritz your cushions, throws, and blankets with the rose water.

- Let the soothing aroma fill your home, making it a safe haven where you can relax during this retrograde.

MARS

Combat any feelings of delayed progress or stalled action during Mars retrograde with these self-care suggestions to help keep you motivated and alert. Affirmations can really make a difference to your daily outlook, so why not try the retrograde ritual at the start of the day to ignite your inner positive energy.

SELF-CARE SUGGESTIONS

- Use the assertive energy of this retrograde to rev up your fitness. Be bold and try a new workout class, or if you prefer to go it alone, change up your running or walking routes. Make exercise a part of your daily routine, even if it's a few stretches first thing to get you fired up.

- Get into self-massage. A mini massage on each hand can calm the mind while continuing to keep you motivated. Use some hand cream and work it into the skin using a circular motion.

- Breathe effectively. Take long, slow breaths when you're feeling stressed and when you need a burst of energy, inhaling deeply through the nose and releasing the air through your lips sharply, as if puffing it out.

RETROGRADE RITUAL

WHAT YOU NEED

A red candle and some matches, a length of red ribbon, and some scissors.

WHAT TO DO

- To begin, light the candle with the matches and position it somewhere that you can see it comfortably.
- Take the length of ribbon and hold it in both hands.
- Gaze into the flame and think about all of the things that you desire. Consider your passions and goals.
- Next, think of any delays or frustrations you might have experienced so far during the retrograde, particularly in relation to these goals. For each one, tie a knot in the ribbon and pull it tight. Imagine pouring all your frustration into the knot as you secure it in place.
- To finish, take the ribbon and cut off each knot, one by one.
- Say, 'Obstacles are opportunities, delays a pause, I move forward with confidence through open doors.'
- Let the candle burn down.

JUPITER

Reflection is key when Jupiter takes a backward spin. It's important to trust your intuition, and take notice of any thoughts and feelings that surface at this time. Use the self-care suggestions and the retrograde ritual to help you get started and tune into those gut instincts and insights.

SELF-CARE SUGGESTIONS

- This planet's retrograde urges you to go within and spend time in quiet contemplation. Make space in your schedule for this, whether you take ten minutes at the start or the end of the day to sit in stillness.

- Get into the habit of journalling how you feel. Pour your emotions onto the page. This will help you de-stress and reflect.

- Boost intuition by holding a piece of amethyst in both hands. Imagine breathing in the vivid purple hue.

RETROGRADE RITUAL

WHAT YOU NEED

Frankincense essential oil, an oil burner, and some space to sit comfortably.

WHAT TO DO

- Add four drops of the essential oil to the water in your oil burner. Frankincense has the ability to help you connect with your intuition and is known for its uplifting properties.

- Close your eyes and take three long, deep breaths so that you inhale the scented vapour.

- Sit comfortably and picture a gold diamond hovering above your head.

- Imagine that for every breath the shimmering diamond gets bigger and brighter, casting light in every direction. See this as an intuitive antenna picking up psychic messages and helping you connect with the wisdom of the Universe.

- Relax and breathe deeply.

- Let any thoughts or insights come to you.

- Picture the golden diamond of light, gradually reducing in size and brightness.

- Open your eyes and give your body a stretch.

SATURN

Life can take a serious turn during a Saturn retrograde, but don't give in to doubts. Instead, call on your core strength by using affirmations and symbols of power and resilience to remind you of your unique gifts. These self-care tips will help focus the mind so that you can move forwards without fear.

SELF-CARE SUGGESTIONS

- The sombre influence of Saturn may challenge you to go within and face your fears. To help, build empowering affirmations into your day by repeating, 'I am strong, I embrace my fear and move on.'
- On waking, visualize a golden cloak of light around you. See it as a cocoon where you are safe and protected from negative energy. At any point during your day, you can reinforce this by picturing the cloak around you.
- Nurture yourself by eating nourishing home-made food at this time.

RETROGRADE RITUAL

WHAT YOU NEED

An hour-glass timer or your smartphone, a piece of paper, and a pen.

WHAT TO DO

- Turn the timer over or set your phone for an hour.
- Sit in quiet reflection and consider where you are right now, and if there is anything holding you back.
- Write down any fears or doubts you have.
- Read through this and reflect on why you feel this way.
- Now consider all of the wonderful qualities and gifts that you have. Write a list of these, then read through them.
- Think of a symbol or simple motif to represent your personal power. It doesn't have to be anything detailed, a circle, sun, or flower design would work. Choose something that resonates with you.
- Continue to trace over the symbol while the timer runs out.
- You might like to draw a copy of the symbol to carry with you as a reminder that you have the power and strength to overcome anything.

URANUS

Embrace the unusual and unexpected shift that comes with a Uranus retrograde, and take this time to think creatively about the future. Exercises that help you develop a flexible attitude and an open mind are essential. Use the retrograde ritual to broaden your perspective, and promote a positive mindset.

SELF-CARE SUGGESTIONS

- This revolutionary retrograde could force you out of your comfort zone. To help expand body and mind and cope with the changes, get into yoga or Pilates. Pushing your body and stretching the limits of movement will keep you mentally stimulated.

- Go on a mindful walk somewhere new. Take in all the sights, sounds, and smells, and connect with the environment.

- Learn something new that challenges the way you experience the world; for example, you might learn a new language or take up an art class.

RETROGRADE RITUAL

WHAT YOU NEED

A clean jar, a piece of clear quartz, lots of bits of paper, and a pen.

WHAT TO DO

- You're going to create a wish jar to promote expansion and help fulfil your potential.

- Place the quartz in the bottom of the jar. Quartz amplifies any energy that you send out, so it works well in manifestation rituals.

- On the pieces of paper, write any hopes, dreams, and wishes that you have. If you're struggling to think of where you'd like to be in a year, three years, five years, and so on, use this as inspiration.

- Screw up the bits of paper into balls and add them to your jar.

- Every morning during the Uranus backspin, give the jar a gentle shake and make a wish for the future.

NEPTUNE

Doubts dissolve during a Neptune backspin, as clarity takes centre stage. This is the time to incorporate self-care tips that focus on clearing the clutter and removing negative thoughts, feelings and practices that block the road forwards. Be bold and let go of what you no longer need with this retrograde ritual.

SELF-CARE SUGGESTIONS

- This planet's reversal brings a hefty dose of reality and the ability to see through the veil to what really matters. To help you flex your organizational skills, clear the clutter. Choose an area in the home, such as your wardrobe or workspace, and eliminate or recycle things you no longer need or use.

- Cleanse your space by burning sage oil or carrying a sage smudge stick around your home and letting the smoke infuse each area.

- Stand beneath the light of the Moon and bathe in its luminescent rays. Imagine they're cleansing you of any negative energy.

RETROGRADE RITUAL

WHAT YOU NEED

A white candle and some matches, a sprig of fresh rosemary, a fireproof bowl, some paper, and a pen.

WHAT TO DO

- Light the white candle and spend a minute watching the flame, to centre yourself. Breathe deeply and relax.
- Place the sprig of rosemary, associated with power and strength, in the fireproof bowl.
- On the paper, write down any negative thoughts or feelings you might have. If something is bothering you, now is the chance to get it off your chest.
- Tear the paper into smaller strips and carefully, one by one, pass them through the flame, then drop them into the bowl to burn.
- Say, 'The veil has dropped, and I am free, I release all doubt so I can see!'
- Let the paper and the rosemary burn, and inhale the smoky fresh aroma.

CONCLUSION

Working with the planets can bring magical energy to your daily routine. It allows you to connect with the Universe on a grand scale and look beyond the mundane, to see the wonder of the world and the cosmos and understand your place in it.

As you align with each planet's power, you'll find it easier to go with the ebb and flow of life's rhythm. You will learn to accept that there is a time for everything and that each phase and planetary movement holds potential for self-development and discovery.

This book provides a starting point from which you can explore; it gives you the basics you need to understand the celestial influences at work. From here you can delve deeper into the night sky, astrology, and any related folklore that captures your interest. You can meditate on what you have uncovered and enjoy the vastness of the world you inhabit. Most importantly, you can appreciate the power of retrograde motion and use it to enhance every aspect of your life.

PLANETS IN RETROGRADE
DIARY

To help you plan ahead for each retrograde, here is a diary which outlines the planets' backward movements over the next five years. This will allow you to prepare for retrograde motion and work with each planet's distinctive energy, as and when it changes. *Please note, these dates are based on Greenwich Mean Time and can fluctuate depending on your local time zone*

2026

	RETROGRADE BEGINS	RETROGRADE ENDS
MERCURY	26 February 29 June 24 October	20 March 23 July 13 November
VENUS	3 October	14 November
MARS	No retrograde this year	
JUPITER	11 November 2025 13 December	11 March 2026 13 April 2027
SATURN	26 July	10 December
URANUS	6 September 2025 10 September	4 February 2026 8 February 2027
NEPTUNE	7 July	12 December

2027

	RETROGRADE BEGINS	RETROGRADE ENDS
MERCURY	9 February 10 June 7 October	3 March 4 July 28 October
VENUS	No retrograde this year	
MARS	10 January	1 April
JUPITER	13 December 2026	13 April 2027
SATURN	9 August	24 December
URANUS	10 September 2026 15 September	8 February 2027 12 February 2028
NEPTUNE	9 July	15 December

2028

	RETROGRADE BEGINS	RETROGRADE ENDS
MERCURY	24 January	14 February
	21 May	14 June
	19 September	11 October
VENUS	10 May	22 June
MARS	No retrograde this year	
JUPITER	12 January	13 May
SATURN	22 August	5 January 2029
URANUS	15 September 2027	12 February 2028
	19 September	16 February 2029
NEPTUNE	11 July	16 December

2029

	RETROGRADE BEGINS	RETROGRADE ENDS
MERCURY	7 January	27 January
	1 May	25 May
	2 September	25 September
	22 December	11 January 2030
VENUS	16 December	26 January 2030
MARS	14 February	5 May
JUPITER	10 February	13 June
SATURN	22 August 2028	5 January 2029
	6 September	19 January 2030
URANUS	19 September 2028	16 February 2029
	23 September	10 February 2030
NEPTUNE	14 July	19 December

2030

	RETROGRADE BEGINS	RETROGRADE ENDS
MERCURY	22 December 2029 13 April 16 August 6 December	11 January 2030 6 May 8 September 25 December
VENUS	16 December 2029	26 January 2030
MARS	No retrograde this year	
JUPITER	13 March	15 July
SATURN	6 September 2029 20 September	19 January 2030 2 February 2031
URANUS	23 September 2029 28 September	20 February 2030 25 February 2031
NEPTUNE	16 July	21 December

FURTHER READING AND RESOURCES

Below you will find a list of interesting books, websites, and apps that will help you further your astrological journey and discover more about the Solar System in general, and also how to identify the planets for yourself.

BOOKS

The Mercury Retrograde Book: Secrets for Surviving and Thriving in Astrology's Most Misunderstood Cycle, by Yasmin Boland (Hay House, 10 May 2022)

Wonders of the Solar System, by Brian Cox (Collins, 30 September 2010)

Turn Left at Orion: Hundreds of Night Sky Objects to see in a Telescope, by Guy Consolmagno, Dan M. Davis (Cambridge University Press, 24 January 2019)

The Story of the Solar System: A Visual Journey, by Dr Maggie Aderin-Pocock, Simon Guerrier (Penguin Books, 26 September 2024)

Stargazing: Beginner's guide to astronomy, by Royal Observatory Greenwich, Radmila Topalovic, Tom Kerss (Collins, 6 October 2016)

The Stories Behind Astrology: Discover the mythology of the zodiac & stars, by Alison Davies (Leaping Hare Press, 29 August 2024)

The Zodiac Year: A Stargazer's Guide to the Astrological Calendar, by Alison Davies (Quadrille Books, 31 October 2024)

WEBSITES

https://science.nasa.gov/solar-system/planets/
https://www.space.com/16080-solar-system-planets.html
https://airandspace.si.edu/explore/stories/our-solar-system
https://gostargazing.co.uk/
https://www.astronomy.com/
https://hubblesite.org/
https://www.retrograde.today/

APPS

Night Sky – Apple device only
Star Walk 2
Stellarium Mobile
Astrology Zone

GLOSSARY

Here is a short glossary, to help you understand fully the meaning of some of the words and terms used within the pages of this book.

Affirmation A positive statement which is said in the present tense and used to create an emotion or outcome.

Ancients Early civilizations.

Aura The invisible energy force field that surrounds the body.

Centred To feel balanced and calm.

Chakra An energy point, often referred to as a 'wheel of energy' situated within the body.

Cosmic Relating to the cosmos or the Universe as a whole.

Guru A spiritual teacher, guide, or mentor.

Infusion A liquid beverage made by infusing herbs and plants in water.

Intuition A sixth sense or gut feeling which comes from within.

Journalling Recording how you feel, by writing in a book known as a journal.

Luna The Latin name for the Earth's Moon, often used as an alternative way to describe its orb.

Manifesting Creating what you want to happen using the power of the mind through your thoughts, visualization, and affirmation.

Mantra A word or sound that is believed to have sacred energy, and is repeated during meditation practice.

Meditation A practice which clears the mind and brings peace, often done by focusing on the journey of the breath.

Mythology A body of myths which belong to a person, culture, or religious group.

Oracle (cards) A set of divinatory cards, which can be used for self-reflection and guidance.

Pantheon A collective group of deities.

Psychic power Abilities that cannot be explained outside of the physical realm.

Ritual A ceremonial or symbolic act which includes words, gestures, and actions.

Scry(ing) A divination practice that involves looking upon a plain or reflective surface to gain insights and visions.

Subconscious A part of the mind that operates below the level of consciousness.

Symbol A mark, image, or character that represents an idea, belief, or emotion.

Third Eye The gateway to intuition and psychic perception, located in the centre of the forehead.

Universe A concept that encompasses everything from space and time to energy and matter.

Visualization The process of picturing something by using the imagination, often used to manifest a desired outcome.

INDEX

A

activities during retrograde 37–45
 things to avoid 38–41
 things to do 42–5
Aquarius
 Mars retrograde 140
 Mercury retrograde 180–1
 Venus retrograde 124
Ariel 81
Aries
 Mars retrograde 130
 Mercury retrograde 160–1
 Venus retrograde 114
Aristotle 7
Assyro-Babylonians 7

B

Babylonians 7, 51, 75
boldness, self-care to help 66–7
breathing exercises 32–3, 41

C

Cancer
 Mars retrograde 133
 Mercury retrograde 166–7
 Venus retrograde 117
Capricorn
 Mars retrograde 139
 Mercury retrograde 178–9
 Venus retrograde 123
Cassini, Giovanni 69
change, self-care to help you face 84–5
clearing your mind ritual 20–1
communication 45
compassion 44
confidence, self-care to boost 102–3
conflict 39–40
confrontation 39–40

D

decision making 39
diary, planets in retrograde 201–6
diet 26–7
dreams
 decoding dreams 31
 dream diaries 30–1

E

emotions, self-care to balance and calm your 96–7
energy
 retrograde energy 18–19
 self-care to help you feel energized 66–7
exercises
 breathing 32–3
 clearing your mind ritual 20–1
 guided meditation 23–5
 journal 28–9
 shifting your perspective 16–17
expressing yourself, with confidence and ease 54–5

F

flexibility 44
focus, self-care to help you to 78–9
food, what to eat 26–7

the future, self-care to help you manifest 72–3

G
Geisel, Theodor Seuss (Dr. Seuss) 51
Gemini
   Mars retrograde 132
   Mercury retrograde 164–5
   Venus retrograde 116
Great Red Spot 69
Greeks 7, 75, 99
guided meditation 23–5

H
Helios 99
horizons, self-care to help you broaden your 72–3

I
intuition, self-care to boost your 90–1

J
journals 28–31
joy, self-care to promote 102–3
Jupiter 68–73
   connecting with the abundant energy of 70
   foods to eat 27
   Jupiter retrograde 144–5, 190–1, 202, 203, 204, 205, 206
   self-care ritual 72–3
   tuning into Jupiter's energy 71

K
Kronos 75

L
Leo
   Mars retrograde 134
   Mercury retrograde 168–9
   Venus retrograde 118
Libra
   Mars retrograde 136
   Mercury retrograde 172–3
   Venus retrograde 120
light, self-care to help you shine your 60–1

M
Mars 15, 62–7
   connecting with the powerful energy of 64
   foods to eat 27
   Mars retrograde 126–41, 188–9, 203, 205
   self-care ritual 66–7
   tuning into Mars' energy 65
meditation, guided 23–5
Mercury 15, 50–5
   connecting with the creative energy of 52
   foods to eat 27
   Mercury retrograde 155, 156–83, 202, 203, 204, 205, 206
   self-care rituals 54–5
   tuning into Mercury's energy 53
the mind, clearing your mind ritual 20–1
the Moon 92–7
   connecting with the intuitive energy of 94

self-care ritual 96–7
tapping into the Moon's energy 95

N
Nabu 51
nature, engaging with 43
Neptune 86–91
    connecting to the imaginative energy of 88
    foods to eat 27
    Neptune retrograde 150–1, 196–7, 202, 203, 204, 205, 206
    self-care ritual 90–1
    tapping into Neptune's energy 89
Ninurta 75

O
Oberon 81
openness 44

P
perspective, shifting your 16–17
Pisces
    Mars retrograde 141
    Mercury retrograde 182–3
    Venus retrograde 125
planets
    planet profiles 46–103
    retrograde planets and your star signs 104–51
    what planet in retrograde means 14–15
    see also individual planets
Plato 7
Pope, Alexander 81
Poseidon 87
projects, launching new 40–1
Prospero 81
psychic awareness, self-care to promote 90–1
Ptolemy 8

R
re-evaluation 45
reflection 45
retrograde energy
    what it does 19
    what it is and what it means for you 18
retrograde motion, preparing for 19
rituals
    clearing your mind ritual 20–1
    Jupiter 70, 72–3, 76, 78–9
    Jupiter retrograde 191
    Mars 64, 66–7
    Mars retrograde 189
    Mercury 52, 54–5
    Mercury retrograde 161, 163, 165, 167, 169, 171, 173, 175, 177, 179, 181, 183
    the Moon 94, 96–7
    Neptune 88, 90–1
    Neptune retrograde 197
    Saturn retrograde 193
    stargazing 34–5
    the Sun 100, 102–3
    Uranus 82, 84–5
    Uranus retrograde 195
    Venus 58, 60–1
    Venus retrograde 187
Romans 7, 57, 63, 75, 99

S

Sagittarius
  Mars retrograde 138
  Mercury retrograde 176-7
  Venus retrograde 122
Sagush 75
Saturn 74-9
  connecting with the protecting energy of 76
  foods to eat 27
  Saturn retrograde 146-7, 192-3, 202, 203, 204, 205, 206
  self-care ritual 78-9
  tapping into Saturn's energy 77
Scorpio
  Mars retrograde 137
  Mercury retrograde 174-5
  Venus retrograde 121
self-esteem, self-care to boost 60-1
Shakespeare, William 81
slowing down 43
Sol Invictus 99
stability, self-care to help 78-9
star signs, retrograde planets and your 104-51
  see also individual star signs
stargazing 34-5
stressing the small stuff 41
the Sun 14, 98-103
  harnessing the vibrant energy of 100
  self-care ritual 102-3
  tapping into the Sun's energy 101

T

Taurus
  Mars retrograde 131
  Mercury retrograde 162-3
  Venus retrograde 115
Titania 81

U

Umbriel 81
the unknown, self-care to help you embrace 84-5
Uranus 80-5
  connecting to the spontaneous energy of 82
  foods to eat 27
  self-care ritual 84-5
  tapping into Uranus' energy 83
  Uranus retrograde 148-9, 194-5, 202, 203, 204, 205, 206

V

Venus 15, 56-61
  connecting with the loving energy of 58
  foods to eat 27
  self-care ritual 60-1
  tuning into Venus' energy 59
  Venus retrograde 110-25, 186-7, 202, 204, 205, 206
Virgo
  Mars retrograde 135
  Mercury retrograde 170-1
  Venus retrograde 119

ACKNOWLEDGEMENTS

I would like to thank my wonderful editor Caitlin Doyle, who gave me the opportunity to work on this, and the entire team at HarperCollins for putting together a beautiful book. I would also like to thank the designer, Sophie Yamamoto, for bringing my words, and the celestial realm to life.

Alison Davies

AUTHOR BIO

Alison Davies is an author, professional storyteller, and freelance writer from Nottingham, UK. She has penned over 60 books, including the popular 'Be More…' series for Quadrille, which started with *Be More Cat* and includes *Be More Bee*, *Be More Sloth*, and *Be More Dog* – one of their top sellers during the pandemic. Other books for Quadrille include *The Mystical Year*, *The Lunar Year*, *The Zodiac Year*, and *The Self Care Year*. More recently *Tales Behind the Tarot* was published by Leaping Hare Press, followed by *Goddess Tales*, *Floral Folklore*, and *The Stories Behind Astrology*. Alison has also written books for Quarto, Bloomsbury, Penguin Random House, Cico, Watkins, and Michael O' Mara Books, and she worked on *The Little Book of Health and Happiness* for the Cath Kidston brand.

When she's not writing books, Alison is a professional storyteller and delivers sessions at universities throughout the East Midlands on how stories can be used as tools for teaching and learning.

Alison's most important and demanding role by far, though, is being cat mum and human of choice to her three furry felines, Ziggy, Diego, and Honey.